The Life of Jesus
Through the eyes of an artist

TEACHER'S GUIDE

David Barton was formerly head teacher of Soho Parish School, and later an education adviser with a specialism in RE. He is an Anglican priest and is currently Warden of The Sisters of the Love of God, an Anglican contemplative community. His wife is the deputy head of a primary school and they live in Oxford, together with their two children.

Jo Fageant is a schools' adviser for the Oxford Diocesan Board of Education. She is also an Ofsted inspector of RE and works as an RE consultant with West Berkshire. She supports schools with their RE planning at both primary and secondary levels and has taught initial teacher training students at both Oxford Brookes and Reading Universities.

Paul Forsey is a full-time artist and designer. He trained in fine art, painting and printmaking at Reading University and is also a qualified teacher of art and design. He has exhibited regularly and has work in many collections including the Arthur Andersen Art Collection, P&O, the Gyosei International College, and a series of ten works on paper in the Strand Headquarters of Enterprise Oil. His religious paintings have been exhibited in church buildings all over England, including Douai Abbey, Sheffield Catholic Cathedral, Lincoln Cathedral, Wells Cathedral and York Minster. If you would like to find out more about Paul's work, please visit www.stepintothepicture.co.uk.

Text copyright © David Barton and Jo Fageant 2004
Illustrations copyright © Paul Forsey 2004

The authors assert the moral right
to be identified as the authors of this work

Published by
The Bible Reading Fellowship
First Floor, Elsfield Hall
15–17 Elsfield Way, Oxford OX2 8FG
ISBN 1 84101 331 5

First published 2004
10 9 8 7 6 5 4 3 2 1 0

Acknowledgments
Scripture quotations are taken from the
Contemporary English Version of the Bible published
by HarperCollins Publishers, copyright © 1991, 1992,
1995 American Bible Society.

A catalogue record for this book is available from the
British Library

Printed and bound in Malta

The Life of Jesus
Through the eyes of an artist
TEACHER'S GUIDE

David Barton with Jo Fageant

ACKNOWLEDGMENTS

Thanks to Danny Sullivan, former Director of Education, Lyn Field and other staff in the Diocesan Board of Education for their inspiration and support. Thanks also to Sue Doggett of BRF for her patience.

THROUGH THE EYES OF AN ARTIST...

Illustrating the Bible is a massive task, particularly as it is the best selling book of all time, although perhaps not the most read! As an artist, I am very interested in pre-Renaissance paintings about both the Old and New Testaments. Their approach to the storytelling is very direct, although some of the details can be hard to draw out. I have experimented with this genre of painting for some years, and this project gave me the opportunity to develop this part of my work. This development is, of course, ongoing.

Initially, although I was aware that the task would be difficult, I was confident that it could be accomplished. As time went on, I was less and less confident (which perhaps is a good thing) and, a little way into the project, I began to realize that this was going to be the biggest creative challenge of my working life so far.

Now that the project is finished, in some ways I feel quite detached from it. As an artist, my hope is that the paintings will embark on a life of their own and, in some small way, create an interest in the extraordinary piece of history that the life of Jesus represents.

Paul Forsey

FOREWORD

This is, quite simply, a brilliant book. Teachers will find it both inspiring and useful and the children who are taught will find material that is both accessible and fun.

In 2000 the Diocese of Oxford commissioned the artist Paul Forsey to produce some illustrations to help families pray the Advent themes. What he produced made an immediate impact. The paintings are vivid, colourful and accessible. This book on the life of Jesus is built around a complete set of paintings by Paul, work that he describes as 'the biggest creative challenge of my working life so far'. Those who look at and use his illustrations will quickly recognize that he has met that challenge.

Using these illustrations, David Barton and Jo Fageant, both extremely experienced in the field of teaching and advising on religious education, have produced material that is fresh and useful.

This version of the life of Jesus is accessible for primary schools and will also extend people's understanding of the narrative. David Barton has provided a commentary on each of the events illustrated, which will help teachers and pupils explore Christian understanding and interpretation. In partnership with Jo Fageant, he has developed lesson plans focused around the paintings and events they illustrate, which will be thought-provoking and fun. They will help pupils both learn about and learn from the life of Jesus. They will also offer appropriate levels of challenge as defined by the QCA level descriptions for RE, thereby enabling teachers to gather evidence of pupils' attainment and progress.

I warmly commend this book, which I believe could prove something of a breakthrough for the teaching of RE.

The Rt Revd Richard Harries, Bishop of Oxford

Contents

Introduction

A FREQUENTLY ASKED QUESTION

What lies behind the biblical accounts of Jesus? Children often ask, 'Is this story true?' It is a question that frequently lingers in the minds of teachers too. Is this literally 'story'— accounts of events that have grown in the telling, or are perhaps simply invented? Or is it history, in the sense of carefully recorded fact?

Before answering that question, it is important to understand how we come to have the story of Jesus in the first place.

How do we know about Jesus?

The life of Jesus is recorded in the four Gospels, which are the first books of the New Testament. Each is titled after its author—Matthew, Mark, Luke and John. Interestingly, although they stand at the beginning of the New Testament, these are not the first pieces of Christian writing. The earliest books are the Epistles, or letters, written by Paul after Jesus' death and resurrection. Paul was converted to Christianity from Judaism by an encounter with the risen Jesus on the road from Jerusalem to Damascus. After this, he travelled around the eastern Mediterranean spreading the teaching of Jesus and establishing Christian communities. Other followers of Jesus did the same.

These early communities grew extraordinarily quickly, even though they soon encountered opposition. They were sustained by their faith, by their powerful sense of community, and by letters of encouragement from their leaders. There was also a strong oral tradition, which passed on the sayings of Jesus and preserved the accounts of his death and resurrection. Over time, these often-told and much-treasured stories became written collections.

It was nearly 30 years before this material was first gathered together and written into a 'life' of Jesus. In a way, the Gospels are books that have been written backwards. The final week of Jesus' life on earth occupies a disproportionately large space in all of them. It was the most frequently recounted set of memories because, for the early Christians (as for contemporary Christians), the death and resurrection of Jesus were the events, above all others, that made clear the nature of God and changed their lives. Before the resurrection, the disciples appear to have heard what Jesus said but never fully understood him. Afterwards, not only did they at last understand, but they lived the message and began to spread it.

Is this history?

When the 'life' of Jesus was written up, it was written, in all four Gospels, in the light of the resurrection. That does not mean that the writers were not concerned about history: they were very much concerned. These accounts are not invention. Luke, one of the Gospel writers, stresses the fact that he is using eyewitness accounts. Looking back in the light of their new understanding, though, they saw that Jesus was not just a teacher with extraordinary authority (which was the way his contemporaries understood him). They had come to understand that his words and actions were those of God. As a result, every remembered event, every detail, became charged with meaning.

Modern biography conditions us to look for objectivity. The Gospel writers are not objective in that sense. Nor are the Gospels a life history in the sense that we would expect. The writers do not appear to be interested in most of Jesus' life before he was 30. Even then, although they record three years of ministry and teaching before Jesus' death, they do not give us enough incidents to fill out the whole of that time. But that was not their concern. They wrote in order to try to help people to understand just who Jesus was, as they understood him, choosing those events that would help them to do so. Had they written these accounts before the resurrection, the Gospels might have turned out differently. As it was, they could not write in any other way than as people who believed that in Jesus they had seen the face of God.

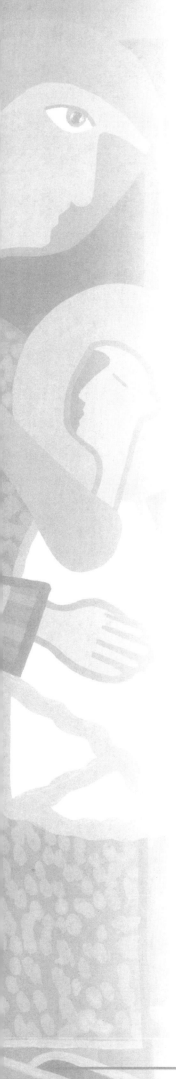

Images and symbols

This means that the imagery and symbolism of the Gospels are very important. In many ways, the technique of the Gospel writers is not unlike that of the artist. They recount a series of events, each of which is like a frozen frame of a very big story—a story so big that words can hardly convey its meaning. Each picture is therefore packed with meaning. Under the surface lies a complex frame of references to other incidents in the Gospel narrative itself and to passages from the Jewish scriptures. We always get far more than is apparent to the casual glance.

The Gospel writers see the world as a place of confrontation between the forces of disorder and chaos on the one hand, and those of truth and goodness in Jesus on the other. This is often expressed by the interplay of darkness and light. It was a time when ordinary people were aware of being powerless, totally unable to influence events. Armies marched over their land; justice was often capricious; illness struck without reason. There was a common perception of the power of these dark collective forces, expressed in the symbolism of evil spirits. Jesus is seen as confronting these spirits and driving them out. His message is that we are not powerless. Each human being is precious.

Jesus appears to have exemplified this in himself: he lived with an extraordinary openness and freedom. The close identification between his words and his deeds is very striking. He *lived* his teaching. There are many things that can be difficult for us now to understand—the miracle stories can puzzle us, for example—but the fact remains that, taking the Gospel record as a whole, Jesus appears to have been someone who had total mastery of his circumstances. His words enabled people to find a new outlook. His actions altered their lives. To encounter him was to encounter someone profound and significant. He left a deep impression on the people of his time—quite beyond those who were close to him. It is all this that the Gospel writers seek to convey.

A story that ends in mystery

Jesus' message was to the Jewish nation as a whole. He had some harsh words to say against the hypocrisy of the leaders of his nation, and clearly his sympathies lay with the poor and the powerless. To them he seemed a potential liberator. The essential thrust of Jesus' teaching was a spiritual one, directed at the recovery of our relationship with God, but it was inevitable that the Roman and the Jewish establishments, smarting under his criticism, would regard his words with suspicion. His popular following in both Galilee and Jerusalem added to their unease. It was this misreading, in the volatile politics of Palestine at the time, that in the end brought about Jesus' death—an end that he had foreseen. The consistency between word and deed that had marked his life was lived out in the final confrontation with cruelty and death.

For the Gospel writers, these events, above all others, reveal Jesus for who he is. Jesus taught that the way to counter evil was by love and forgiveness, and in the long hours of his trial and death, he was utterly faithful to that teaching. His affirmation of love, even in these extreme circumstances, points beyond the known into the unknown, and here the Gospel writers (as well as contemporary Christians) are unashamed in their inability to explain. The resurrection remains a mystery, but a mystery that is understood in the experience of changed lives and the ability to emulate at least something of who Jesus was. It was—and is—a way of living that turns our usual expectations upside down. Life emerges from weakness and apparent failure, from the place of the victim, and not from success and power. A pointer to the meaning of the resurrection is that the confused and frightened disciples found themselves overwhelmingly grasped by this truth. Their boldness after the resurrection of Jesus was remarkable.

Using material from the Bible

This, then, is the experience and understanding that underpins the Gospels and indeed the whole New Testament, shaping the vocabulary of the writers and the images they use. It creates a subject matter very different from that used in other areas of the humanities curriculum. Teachers who use this material will need to find their own ways of relating to it.

All religious story (from all religious traditions) challenges and confronts—that is its nature—and Jesus' way of making people look at the world in a totally different light is reflected in every word and incident of his life. Inevitably this is reflected in all of the material used in this book. But the teacher is not evangelizing, and there is always a way in which both teacher and class can use the stories and their accompanying pictures simply to ponder and reflect in an open-ended manner. At one level, that will allow children to grasp the story of someone who has profoundly influenced Western history—and beyond. The material can also be used to reflect on the ways in which we relate to each other and to those who might seem 'different' in ways we do not understand. There are questions about the values we hold, and our attitudes towards other people. At another level, this material can be used to help children see that life is infinitely more profound than they might have imagined. The events and stories ask us to *think*, and to re-examine the assumptions on which we base our actions. If that level of seriousness can be achieved, the teacher should be content.

All of this is greatly helped by the ability simply to look at the picture and respond to what the detail tells the viewer. The pictures use symbols and related events to extend the narrative—a method that echoes the way the Gospels themselves are written.

HOW TO USE THIS BOOK

The material is organized in three sections, each designed to help draw out the significance and symbolism of the story alongside the artist's own interpretation.

Complementary narratives

The three narratives are written as a complement to the biblical text of the accompanying book. They will best be heard by showing the pictures alongside the narrative, in the hope that this will allow the children to approach the biblical text with greater ease. Narrative forms a key part of Christian understanding, and this is particularly true of the accounts of the last week of Jesus' life. Too often, children (and adults) have only a partial grasp of these events. Reading the continuous story first, while referring to the pictures, will allow a later return to specific events without confusion.

Accompanying notes

The accompanying notes will help teachers to flesh out the story or event. Children will develop their own ability to 'read' the symbolism, and this, if it is encouraged, will be an important part of the interpretation that can be shared among the class.

Each picture is given supporting material, so that the background of each event can be fully explored before a lesson is developed. The 'Artist's eye' allows both teachers and children to view each scene from the perspective of someone who has come to the material with a fresh eye, which may stimulate children to make their own responses to the events described. Throughout the teaching material, very little is said about a response in terms of artistic appreciation, because that is the obvious option. Those of us who have worked on this book hope that the paintings will be a stimulus towards new and original responses by children. Often, the 'eye' of a child sees meaning that eludes an adult. If this book can stimulate such responses, it will have done its work.

Lesson planning guides

The lesson plans are divided between Lower and Upper Key Stage 2. In approaching them, teachers will need to be aware of the aim of the unit and its key questions. It will be important to have the pictures referred to available as a focus for the lesson. The material is designed to help pupils learn *about* the events of Jesus' life and their religious significance, and also to help them reflect on their own experiences in the light of what they have learned. A number of the lessons depend on a discussion among the class as a whole, and teachers will need to prepare for this in advance by reading the supportive pages for the pictures as well as the lesson plans. At some key moments (for example, in the lesson about the healing miracle, pp. 82), we have tried to be clear

about what a Christian view might be, so that teachers can be confident in leading the discussion. Further activities are suggested and, in some cases (though not all), worksheets have been provided.

Although it is important for pupils to learn about the life of Christ and the events that point towards Christian faith, there is a focus throughout these lessons on mystery and wonder. Within the limitations of planning, we have tried to open children's eyes to a large and wonderful world around them. We attempt to capture some of the essence of Jesus' teaching that even the humdrum and ordinary is charged with glory and grandeur—it is a search for the poetry of life beyond the prose. This means that a number of questions will need to be left open. It is what we ask that matters, rather than our answers. If teachers can convey some of this, much will have been achieved.

At the end of a unit, teachers are encouraged to make an assessment of pupils' learning in the light of the assessment questions provided, which have been drawn from the QCA Level Descriptions for RE. It will be important for all teachers to become familiar with these questions.

Complementary narratives

The story of Jesus (Part One)

This is the story of someone who lived 2,000 years ago. He died when he was only 33 years old. He lived in a small country in a remote area, and never travelled anywhere else. Most of what we know about him comes from only three years of his life. Yet he is one of the most important people in history. Even today, when a lot of people don't know much about him, we still have a holiday and give each other presents to mark the time of his birth—and we remember the end of his life too. His name is Jesus of Nazareth.

EVENT 1

The birth of Jesus is announced

LUKE 1:26–31

The story of Jesus begins nine months before he was born. Mary, his mother, was engaged to a man called Joseph. One day, Mary was visited by an angel, who told her that she would have a son. Mary was startled. It was not what she expected. Joseph too had a dream. The angel told him that when the boy was born he should be called Jesus. The name means 'someone who will save people'.

Joseph dreams

MATTHEW 1:18–21

For Mary and Joseph, all of this was strange. Joseph was a carpenter. Mary, who was not yet his wife, was still young. They did not think of themselves as important people, but they both felt that they had been visited by the spirit of God. What did this mean? All they could do was to accept what had happened, and wait and see.

EVENT 2

The birth of Jesus

LUKE 2:1–19

When a baby is about to be born, everyone makes careful preparations. The mother of the baby makes sure she has plenty of rest and quiet. But for Mary, waiting for Jesus' birth, that was not possible. Far away in Rome, the emperor decided that he wanted to know how many people he had in his empire, so he ordered that each family had to go to their father's birthplace to be counted. Joseph came from Bethlehem, which was several days' walk away from Nazareth. They had to go. It was dangerous for a pregnant woman, but more dangerous not to do it—the Romans were harsh with people who disobeyed.

So Mary and Joseph went to Bethlehem. The town was full with all the other people who had gone to be counted. The only place where they could stay was in a stable. It was not very clean, but it was warm. There Jesus was born.

The birth of every baby is wonderful. Mary held her child close, then wrapped him warmly and put him in the trough that was used for feeding the animals. She and Joseph gazed and gazed at Jesus. As they watched and he slept, it was as if the stable was filled with light, and again they sensed that they were surrounded and protected by the spirit of God. They had wanted so much more for Jesus—a clean room, a proper house—but it did not matter. He and they would be safe. They were in God's hands—they knew it. Never before had they felt so much happiness.

EVENT 3

The wise men

MATTHEW 2:1–12

Before they could return to Nazareth, Mary had to recover from the birth. While she waited and rested, they had visitors. There were some shepherds who came from the fields outside Bethlehem. They said they had been woken by angels during the night, who told them of Jesus' birth. The baby was to be someone very important for them and for everyone. The shepherds were simple, ordinary people. They knelt and looked at the sleeping child, and then quietly went on their way.

There were some other visitors. They were very different—travellers who looked at the stars. They came, they said, from far away. They had seen a new star which meant that a new, important baby, perhaps a future ruler, had been born. They brought gifts to honour him—rich presents of gold, frankincense and myrrh.

As they gave the gifts, Mary's heart felt a stab of pain. The gifts, she knew, meant danger to her tiny son. Gold was for a king—but to become a king in that world was risky. Frankincense was used in the temple as people prayed—why was this given to Jesus? And myrrh… it was used when people died and their bodies were put in the grave. Her heart went cold, and she held Jesus close.

EVENT 4

The killing of the children

MATTHEW 2:16–18

When the travellers had first seen their star and understood that someone important was to be born, they had expected that such a person would be found in a royal palace. So, arriving in the land where Jesus was, they first went to visit King Herod. Now Herod had no

children, and when he heard about a possible new ruler, he was very suspicious. He was also very cunning. He brought together the chief priests and teachers of the Jewish Law (of Moses) and asked them where a future ruler might be born. They told him that the most likely place would be Bethlehem, so he told the travellers and sent them on their way, asking them to come back and tell him where this baby was. He said that he too would like to pay a visit.

After they had visited Mary, Joseph and Jesus, the travellers had a dream. 'Avoid Herod,' an angel said, so they went home another way. But that did not stop Herod. He sent his soldiers to Bethlehem with orders to kill all the boy children who were about Jesus' age. It was a terrible thing. The sound of crying filled the town. Joseph, however, had also been warned in a dream. He led Jesus and Mary to a safe place.

EVENT 5

Simeon praises the Lord

LUKE 2:22–35

There was a special duty to be done. Mary and Joseph had to take Jesus to the temple in Jerusalem to give thanks to God. The temple was a place of great beauty. Its walls were covered in gold, and people brought many expensive gifts to make it more beautiful. Mary and Joseph could only afford very simple presents—two young doves—but their hearts were full of thankfulness.

There were two people in the temple who had been there many years. Their names were Simeon and Anna. Both were very old. They loved the temple very much, but they had seen things they did not like to remember—cruel soldiers entering this holy place and killing the priests; ordinary people, hungry and frightened. So now they stayed in the temple to pray to God for help.

When Mary and Joseph came shyly into the temple courtyard, carefully holding Jesus to keep him safe, Simeon and Anna knew that there was something very important about this child. It was as if a light suddenly cleared away the darkness. They had seen many families come to say 'thank you' for their children, but none had brought a child like this. They ran to Mary and Joseph, laughing and singing. 'This is the child!' Simeon said. 'This is the one we have been waiting for! He will be a light for the world!'

It was such a commotion. Mary and Joseph did not know what to think, but Mary feared for Jesus again. Simeon spoke of light, but it was as if a shadow fell across her son. Her heart ached for him.

EVENT 6

The boy Jesus in the temple
LUKE 2:41–52

There is one final thing we know about Jesus. As a young person, aged twelve, his parents took him to the temple in Jerusalem again, this time from Nazareth. When they left the city

to go home, Jesus was not with them. They were not bothered: he often played with friends, and they were with a large crowd. Jesus would be safe, they thought—following behind with other children. But after a while they realized he was not there at all. He was lost.

Anxiously they went back to Jerusalem, looking everywhere they had been. They found him in the temple. He was sitting and talking with some of the wisest people in the city. He was happy in this circle of teachers, and they were amazed

at his learning. Mary was anxious and cross. 'We have been looking everywhere for you,' she said. Jesus might have wanted to stay. He loved the temple. But he went back with them to Nazareth, and for the next 20 years or so we hear nothing about him. One day he would return to the temple, for a very different visit.

The story of Jesus (Part Two)

EVENT 7

The baptism of Jesus
MATTHEW 3:13–17

Many years later, a strange man walked out of the desert. He wore animal skins and ate the food of the desert—insects and the honey from wild bees. His name was John.

As John walked through the towns and villages, he was shocked. People took no notice of God's commands. They only thought about themselves. There was lying and cheating. The rich became richer and the poor became poorer. 'You are all like snakes, eating one another,' John said. 'Change your ways.'

John went to the River Jordan. Jordan is in a deep valley, and in a dry land its water gives life to many trees and plants. John stood in the middle of the river, and those who had heard what he said, and were ready to change their ways, entered the water and came and stood in front of him. John dipped them under the water, one by one. When people came out of the river, they felt as if they had washed off their old ways. Now they would lead better lives. Great crowds came to be baptized like this. John was making a difference.

Then Jesus came and stood in front of John. They were cousins, and John knew that Jesus was a good person. 'Not you,' John said. 'You should baptize me.'

'No,' said Jesus. 'It is right that I should be baptized.' So John began to pour the water over Jesus' head, and at that moment it seemed as if heaven opened and the spirit of God came down on Jesus. A voice came from heaven saying, 'You are my Son.'

Jesus walked out of the water and, without another word, went into the desert.

but never listened to. That was not the way.

Then it was as if he was on a high mountain, with all the cities of the world in view. Beside him was someone who whispered to him about getting an army and conquering them all. Then he would have the power to rule with peace and fairness, as no one else had done. Jesus looked at the person who whispered to him, and he saw the cruel eyes, the sharp knives of evil. He thought of the armies and the killing as his kingdom was made. 'Get behind me,' he said. 'I am not following your temptations.'

Jesus walked out of the desert. He would be just who he had always been—ordinary, like everyone else. But he would allow the love of God to tell him what to do and what to say. He would listen to nothing else.

EVENT 8

The temptations of Jesus

MATTHEW 4:1–11

The desert is dry and empty, a lonely place, but it is a place to think, and Jesus needed to think. What should he do now? He knew he was being asked by God to do something special for the people of his land and, beyond them, for many others too. But what was he to do?

Perhaps he should provide food for people—so many were hungry. No one had ever done it, but he knew he could. It would be like turning stones into bread. But to do that he needed power, and

when he thought of that, Jesus knew something was wrong. He saw red eyes of greed and envy. No. That was not the way.

Perhaps he should go to the temple he loved. Perhaps there people would listen to him. He saw himself with the crowds pressing round—he could attract so many people. But he saw how proud and comfortable he could become—someone people worshipped

EVENT 9

Jesus chooses his first disciples

LUKE 5:1–11

Not long afterwards, Jesus was walking by Lake Galilee. Already people were following him. Whenever he spoke, people sat down to listen. Somehow, listening to him helped them to understand life better. Today there were so many people that no one could see him. There was a boat pulled up on the shore, and the fishermen were sitting, mending their nets beside it. Jesus jumped into the boat and, sitting on the end of it, a little way out from the bank, he spoke to the crowds sitting on the shore.

When he had finished, he turned to the fisherman. 'Let's go fishing,' he said. The fisherman was called Simon Peter. 'Master,' Simon Peter said. 'We have been fishing all night and caught nothing. But if you say so, we'll go.'

No one fished by daylight, but still, they

rowed out into the middle of the lake and put out the nets. All at once, the nets were full of fish—so many that it was impossible to pull them on board, and the nets threatened to break. Simon had no time to think. Desperately he signed to his friends in another boat to come and help, and with both boats at sinking point they rowed slowly to the shore.

Never had Simon had such a catch! It was huge. What was it about Jesus that had caused this to happen? Simon fell to his knees, amazed and half afraid. So did his friends James and John, but Jesus said, 'Do not be afraid. Follow me. I need your help.'

To their own surprise and the surprise of their friends, Simon Peter, James and John left everything—their boats, their families, their homes—and followed Jesus.

EVENT 10

Jesus heals a man

MATTHEW 8:1–4

Jesus was always followed by crowds. Often he would stop and speak to them, and his words are words that have always been remembered.

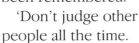

'Don't judge other people all the time. Look at yourself: are you always good? Put yourself right before you start to put other people right.'

'Forgive each other.'

'Love your enemies. God accepts people just as they are. You must do the same.'

'Always treat other people as you would like to be treated yourself. Make that your rule.'

Often after he had spoken like this, people who were sick came to him. One man came, covered in sores. To have this illness was to be very lonely. People avoided you in case they too caught the disease. When the man moved forward, everyone backed away, but Jesus accepted him just as he was.

The man knelt. 'Lord, you can make me clean,' he said.

'I can,' said Jesus. 'Be clean.'

The man was clean, from that moment. 'Go and show the priests you are clean,' said Jesus, 'and then go home.'

Everyone was amazed.

EVENT 11

Jesus calms a storm

LUKE 8:22–25

Another thing that Jesus taught people was not to worry.

'Don't worry about your life. Don't be anxious,' he said. 'God will look after you. Trust God and everything else will work out.'

One day, Jesus got into a boat with his disciples to cross Lake Galilee. It had been a long day, with many people crowding around. Jesus was tired. He lay down on the cushions at the end of the boat and at once fell deeply asleep. As they went across the lake, the wind became stronger. Before they could reach the other side, it had blown into a storm. The disciples were good sailors, but this storm was bigger than they could manage. The water was filling the boat faster than they could bail it out. In their panic they had forgotten about Jesus, but now they woke him. 'Master! We are lost!' they shouted.

Jesus woke, stood up in the boat and looked around him. As he gazed on to the grey, rough water, it was as if the storm suddenly and quietly came to an end, and everything became still. 'Where is your faith?' he asked. 'Where is your trust in God?'

Afterwards the disciples could not forget what had happened. It was almost as if the wind and the waves had obeyed Jesus.

EVENT 12

Jesus feeds five thousand

MATTHEW 14:13–21

Jesus spent three years walking round Palestine, teaching and healing. People came from far and near to hear him, and he turned no one away. Ordinary people loved him because his words made sense to them, and he practised what he preached. He spoke of God as a God of love—a God who is like a shepherd, searching out sheep that get lost and bringing them home safely. When people were close to Jesus, it was as if they could see the love of God he spoke about, turned towards them in Jesus' face.

But these were not easy times. The Romans ruled Palestine, and no one liked them. There were always rebellions or rumours of rebellions, and suspicion everywhere. Anyone who was popular, and liked by the crowds, was seen by the Romans and even by the Jewish leaders as someone who might cause trouble.

At about this time, Jesus' cousin John was thrown into prison by King Herod. John was a good man, but he had criticized the king, and in the end Herod put him to death. When Jesus heard of John's death, he got into a boat and went to a desert place—the kind of place that John came from—to be alone. He wanted to mourn, and perhaps he wondered what the death of John might mean for him.

But Jesus did not have time to be alone. The crowds followed him round the lake. Many people stood waiting for him on the shore. Perhaps they wondered if God was involved in all this cruelty.

Jesus always taught that God had no part in the way we treat each other. Once he told the story of a young man who left home and spent half of his father's money. When he returned, he expected anger and punishment, but he found his father waiting for him, running to meet him, glad and happy to see him. He was loved and welcomed home with a rich feast. God waits for us in the same way, Jesus taught. With God, we are always welcome.

Jesus spoke to the crowd for a long time. Towards evening, the disciples wanted to send everyone away, as the people were hungry. But Jesus asked what food there was to give them. 'Just five small loaves of bread and two small fish,' the disciples said. 'It is nowhere near enough for so many.'

'Bring it all to me,' said Jesus. He took the bread and fish, held them up to God and blessed them. Then he gave the food to the disciples and told them to share it between everyone. There were five thousand people out there in the desert, but, in a way that no one understood, everyone had enough to eat. There was even food left over. People had come feeling anxious and worried, but now they went home feeling better and stronger. It was as if they had shared the feast of welcome Jesus had spoken about.

EVENT 13

The true glory of Jesus

LUKE 9:28–36

From now on, Jesus seems to have understood that what had happened to John might well happen to him. He tried to tell this to his friends, the disciples, but they did not want to hear. 'Don't speak of it,' Peter said.

Then Jesus took Peter and John and James with him to the top of a mountain. It was a wonderful place. They sat together in silent prayer, high above the valley, the light all around them. They seemed far away from the sadness about John, and Jesus' talk about what might happen to him. As they prayed, the light become stronger and, while Peter, James and John looked on, they saw Jesus shining—his face changed and his clothes sparkling white. There were two men with him, two people from the past—Moses, the great lawgiver, and Elijah, the great prophet. They seemed to be talking with Jesus about what might happen to him in Jerusalem.

As they spoke, the light shone as they had never seen light before. Then Moses and Elijah began to leave. Peter could not bear this wonderful moment to end. 'Master, this is wonderful,' he said. 'Stay, and we will make three shelters for you!' But as he spoke, a cloud overshadowed the light and the voice of God came from the cloud: 'This is my Son. Listen to him.'

It was after this that Jesus began to get ready to go to Jerusalem.

The story of Holy Week and Easter

It was spring, and the weather was getting warmer. Soon it would be the Festival of Passover. Passover was the most important of the year's many festivals, and all Jews longed to spend Passover in the holy city of Jerusalem and to pray in the temple. Jesus decided to go to Jerusalem too. He gathered his disciples with him and set out on the long walk through the mountains.

Jesus knew that it would not be easy to visit Jerusalem. Passover was a celebration of freedom—the freedom that his people once found when they escaped from being slaves in Egypt. After 40 years in the desert, they had come here to the land and to the city of Jerusalem, given to them by God, but now they were no longer free.

Many people wanted Jesus to be the leader who would once more set them free from foreign rule. He had been asked many times, and many times he had made it clear that he would have nothing to do with such a struggle. The freedom Jesus spoke of was different. But people's hopes did not go away. The danger was that if Jesus went to Jerusalem, the crowds, excited by the festival, would try to turn him into some sort of king. If that happened, the chief priests, and behind them the Romans, would be quick to turn on Jesus, and if the crowd were disappointed, they could be unpleasant too.

Still, Jesus decided to go. He felt the need to be in Jerusalem, the city he loved. On the way he tried to warn his disciples of the danger. He was not going to change what he said. He was not going to be popular with anyone, and he was not going to hide. But the disciples still could not understand. They could not imagine that anyone would not love Jesus as they did.

EVENT 14

Jesus enters Jerusalem

MATTHEW 21:1–11

When they arrived in the villages outside Jerusalem, it was clear that everyone knew Jesus was coming. The crowds were excited. Was this the hoped-for moment? Jesus had an answer. There was a prophecy about a very different sort of king—a humble king who rode a donkey. No one who rides a donkey could possibly be trying to lead people to war with the Romans. The Romans had a large army with great chariots and war horses.

So Jesus rode into Jerusalem on a quiet and gentle donkey, but the crowds went wild just the same. They came pouring out of the gates, pulling down palm branches to wave, and putting their coats in front of the donkey. 'Hosanna to the Son of David!' they shouted.

In the confusion, Jesus slipped off the donkey and disappeared.

Later, when the crowd had gone, Jesus went into the temple to pray. He was shocked and sad. The beautiful temple of God had become more like a market than a place in which to pray. Angry, Jesus turned over the tables of the money changers, and chased them all out. 'This should be a house of prayer, not a den of thieves!' he said. The priests were furious. After that, they plotted how they could arrest him.

EVENT 15

Jesus washes the feet of his disciples

JOHN 13:4–12

In the week of Passover, friends often met together for a meal, when they would remember the story of their ancestors' escape from Egypt. On Thursday, Jesus arranged such a meal with his friends. It was held in an upstairs room.

When everything was ready and the disciples had all arrived, Jesus knelt down and began to wash their feet. The disciples were surprised. Rich people had slaves to do this—it was not the job of a great teacher. 'No, Lord,' said Peter. 'You cannot wash my feet.' But Jesus insisted, and as he went round, washing their feet one by one, the disciples began to realize how much he cared for them all. He loved them so much that he was even prepared to do *this*! 'This is how I want you to care for each other,' he said to them afterwards.

EVENT 16

The Lord's Supper

MATTHEW 26:20–30

Then they ate a meal together. At the end, Jesus took bread and wine. 'Whenever

you eat and drink like this,' he said, 'do it to remember me.' He broke the bread and handed it to them. He passed round the cup. As they ate that meal with him, they felt closer to him than they ever had before, and they knew that it was something they would never forget.

After the meal, Jesus looked at Judas. Judas shifted in his seat and looked uncomfortable. 'Do what you have to do,' Jesus said quietly. Judas got up and went out.

Judas was a traitor. Earlier in the week he had gone to the chief priests and had told them that if they paid him, he would betray Jesus. Now he went and told them where Jesus was. 'Soon he will go to Gethsemane to pray,' he said. 'You can arrest him there. It is away from the crowds.' The priests paid him 30 pieces of silver.

EVENT 17

Jesus is arrested

MATTHEW 26:47–56

After the meal, Jesus went to the garden of Gethsemane. He knew what would happen, and his prayer was troubled. Among the trees the disciples struggled to keep awake.

Suddenly the garden was full of noise and soldiers and lights. Out of the shadows stepped Judas. 'Master,' he said, and ran forward and kissed Jesus. It was a signal. Immediately the soldiers ran to Jesus and arrested him. Jesus looked at Judas. 'Judas,' he said, 'do you betray me with a kiss?'

Peter suddenly sprang forward. From somewhere he pulled out a sword and struck out, cutting the ear of one of the soldiers. 'Put away your sword,' said Jesus.

'People who use swords will die by them.' He reached out his hand and healed the man's ear.

Then Jesus was led away. Fearing for their lives too, the disciples ran away and went into hiding.

EVENT 18

Pilate questions Jesus

MATTHEW 27:11–26

First Jesus was taken to Caiaphas, the high priest, who had collected together the whole council of priests. Caiaphas wanted Jesus dead. He had paid some people to give false evidence against Jesus, but they were not much help: their story was muddled. After a confusing discussion, Caiaphas sent them away and glared at Jesus. 'Are you the Son of God?' he shouted. 'If you say so,' replied Jesus. That was enough for Caiaphas. 'Blasphemy!' he shouted. All the others agreed. 'Jesus deserves death,' they said.

Caiaphas now had to take Jesus to Pilate, the Roman governor. Only Pilate could decide whether someone should be condemned to death or not. Caiaphas knew that Pilate would make up his own mind. He might not accept that Jesus should die. So Caiaphas sent some of his servants to join the crowd outside the governor's palace, with secret instructions, just in case.

When Pilate heard the charges against a man who had never caused him any trouble before, he was suspicious—and he was worried. Jesus had been loved by the crowds. There was a danger that they might now cause a riot on his behalf, and Pilate was anxious to avoid trouble at the time of Passover.

To make matters more difficult, Pilate's wife came to see him while he was thinking about this. 'Take care of that man Jesus,' she said. 'I have dreamt about him this morning, and he is good.'

So Pilate looked for a way out. Usually at Passover he freed a prisoner, as a mark of respect for the festival. If this year he asked the crowds to choose between Jesus and another man, called Jesus Barabbas, who had been a murderer, the people would be bound to choose Jesus of Nazareth. Then Jesus could be freed, the high priest could be ignored, and trouble would be avoided.

Ignoring Caiaphas, Pilate walked over to the window and stood in front of the crowds waiting outside. 'Who would you like me to release to you this year?' he shouted. 'Jesus of Nazareth, or Jesus Barabbas?'

Caiaphas was ready for that idea. His servants were in the crowd, and they did the job they were paid to do. 'Release Jesus Barabbas!' they shouted. There was much noise and confusion. No one understood what was going on. Pilate could not hear. He tried again. 'Who should I release? Jesus of Nazareth, or Jesus Barabbas?' The voices shouted up again: 'Release Jesus Barabbas!' Once more Pilate tried, and the voices of the high priest's servants came out above all the others: 'Release Jesus Barabbas!'

Pilate walked back from the window, knowing that he had been tricked. But if this meant that the priests were prepared to encourage a riot during the festival, he had better take notice. A riot, for whatever reason, was the last thing he needed. He called for a bowl of water and washed his hands. 'It is nothing to do with me,' he said. Then he condemned Jesus to die on a cross.

Jesus was taken downstairs to the soldiers' hall, and there the soldiers beat him with a whip. They put a crown of thorns on his head, and mocked and bullied him about being a king. Then, tired and exhausted already, Jesus was given the heavy wooden bar that would be part of his cross, and was told to start walking.

EVENT 19

Jesus is nailed to a cross

MATTHEW 27:31–54

It was a long journey, through streets where people either wept or shouted insults. Jesus fell so many times that the soldiers ordered a man from the crowd to carry the bar of his cross to the place of crucifixion, while Jesus stumbled along behind.

When they got there, two other men were brought to be crucified. Three crosses, on a lonely hill; three men in great pain, waiting to die. In the distance a small crowd watched, wondering if this would be the moment when a heavenly army came to rescue this good man. But nothing happened—and when nothing happened, there were jeers and shouts and insults. Close to the cross, Jesus' mother Mary, his disciple John and a few other women watched, weeping. There was nothing they could do, but they stayed close. By the cross, the soldiers kept guard.

Every now and then, they heard Jesus' voice. He was reciting the words of a song to himself, a song he had known since childhood—'My God, my God, why have you forgotten me?'—just that. He could have shouted out in pain. He could have sworn at the soldiers as the other prisoners did when the nails were driven in. Instead it was as if he asked God to forgive them, and now, on the cross, his mind seemed to be lost in prayer to God.

After three long hours, Jesus asked for a drink. A soldier reached up with a sponge soaked in sour wine, stuck on the end of a spear. He put it to Jesus' lips.

Then Jesus gave a loud cry and died.

Afterwards, when the disciples came to talk of Jesus' death, they said that it was as if the whole world wept at this moment. The sky darkened, the earth shook, and a great curtain in the temple was torn from top to bottom.

Jesus' family and a few friends took his body from the cross and put it into a tomb for burial. The tomb had been carved from the rock and a great stone was rolled across the entrance. The chief priests were worried that Jesus' body might be stolen, so they sent guards to keep his disciples away.

EVENT 20

Jesus is alive

MARK 16:1–8

Two days later, when Passover was finished, three women came to the tomb to remember Jesus. They brought spices to put beside his body, as was the custom. As they came to the place, they remembered the great stone blocking the entrance, and wondered what to do. But

when they looked, they saw that the huge stone had been rolled away and the guards were gone. Amazed, they went into the tomb, and there they saw a young man in white. 'Jesus is not here. He is risen,' said the man. 'You will see him. Go and look.'

The women stumbled out of the tomb, both happy and afraid. After that, they and the other disciples looked, and saw Jesus, risen, just as they had been told.

Then some disciples saw him in Galilee, in the place where they had heard him teaching. Two other disciples saw him in a village outside Jerusalem. They shared a meal with a stranger who had spoken to them, and as he broke the bread they knew it was Jesus.

EVENT 21

Jesus and Thomas

JOHN 20:24–29

One day, while the disciples were eating a meal in the room where they had eaten that final meal before his arrest, Jesus was suddenly among them again. He was alive. Each time they saw him he seemed alive with a life that made them feel strong, not frightened. It puzzled them and strengthened them at the same time.

Thomas did not see Jesus in that upstairs room like the others. When they told him, Thomas remembered the cross. 'It cannot be him,' he said. 'I remember the wounds on his hands and feet too well.' A week later, in the same place, Jesus appeared to Thomas. His body was wounded, but Jesus was alive. Thomas knew as he looked that this was a life that could only have come from God. 'My Lord and my God!' he said.

From then on, everything changed. The cross that had once seemed to be the end now became the beginning. It was as if Jesus had become part of the life of his friends, and at the same time had changed the whole world. Once they had been frightened and run away; now they feared nothing. Once the world had seemed so dark; now it was full of light. They were glad to be alive. There were so many possibilities.

EVENT 22
The coming of the Holy Spirit
ACTS 2:1–12

Not long afterwards, the disciples were all together in a house. Suddenly they knew, without any doubt, that everyone had to be told this story. From now on, that was what they must do. It was as if the Spirit of God, which they had seen in Jesus, was now in them too, so they walked out and simply told people what they had heard and seen. The people who heard told others, and that is how, 2,000 years later, we can tell the story and understand what they understood.

Accompanying notes

The story of Jesus (Part One)

EVENT 1
The birth of Jesus is announced
LUKE 1:26–31

Joseph dreams
MATTHEW 1:18–21

 Background

The stories of Jesus' birth take us into an unexpected world. It is a world visited by angels, where people take notice of their dreams and burst unexpectedly into song. This is not our world. But the writer wants us to have a particular awareness. The story we are being told cannot be easily explained. It can be understood only if people have a sense of the mystery of life, and if they understand that by searching below its surface, we can see beauty and wonder. Everything in the story points beyond itself to the vast immensity that we dare to call God. To see this world, we have to have the eye of a poet or an artist. We have to be ready to be surprised and knocked off our feet.

Gabriel makes clear that something new and unexpected is about to happen. Mary is to give birth to a child who will be alive with the life of God. Mary does not understand what this means; nor does Joseph, and nor do we.

The birth of Jesus could mean embarrassment. Mary is only engaged to Joseph; they are not married, nor do they live together. It is likely that she would have been quite young at this time and he a much older man. But Mary and Joseph do not dismiss Gabriel's message. They simply trust and accept. They allow their eyes to be opened to a whole new way of looking at life. Even more than that, because Mary says 'Yes', the whole of the rest of the story can unfold—a story that is going to bring wonder, challenge and surprise to everyone.

 About the picture

Gabriel is shown in a doorway, or frame, as if it were an entry into another world—the kingdom of God. Note that it is marked out as different from, yet recognizably still part of, this world: the landscape is seen again through the door. Jesus spoke of God's kingdom as being 'here and now'.

Gabriel reaches out to offer Mary a flower, a symbol of life—in this case, the life of God. The same life is symbolized by the dove at the top of the picture—the

traditional Christian symbol for the Holy Spirit. At the bottom, Joseph, in his carpenter's apron, sleeps, reminding us of his dream in which Gabriel tells him of his own responsibility to protect Mary and Jesus. Mary carries a bag, perhaps telling us that she is a working woman.

 Artist's eye

When I first painted the annunciation, I only showed the exchange between Mary and Gabriel, but with hindsight I was unhappy about the absence of Joseph from the painting. The separate appearance of the angel Gabriel to Joseph in a dream is also important, as it is not only Mary's life that changes direction. The faith that Joseph subsequently displays reinforces the significance of this incident. I see Mary as a scared teenager with events thrust upon her, and Joseph's loyalty is crucial.

Gabriel passes Mary the gift of life in the form of a flower, while Joseph sleeps peacefully and dreams in the reassurance that he is right to stand by Mary in her predicament.

 Looking at the picture

◈ Who is the focus of attention in this picture ?

◈ How are Mary and the angel marked out as special?

◈ What would make you think that this story might be telling us something about God?

◈ What does Joseph's clothing tell us about his work?

◈ Why are flowers special, and when do we give them to people?

EVENT 2

The birth of Jesus

LUKE 2:1–19

 Background

The surprising story continues: a baby is born. But we are to look carefully, because this is no ordinary baby. Luke is careful to place the birth of Jesus in the context of history—in the reign of Caesar Augustus. This is not recorded in Matthew, who mentions only King Herod, the local ruler. It is from Luke, not Matthew, that we get the idea of a journey by Mary and Joseph from Nazareth to Bethlehem on account of the census, as well as the idea of a stable (or perhaps a temporary caravanserai) because of the overcrowded inn.

Throughout his Gospel, Luke is concerned to show that Jesus is alongside the poor people of his time, and this is emphasized by the makeshift nature of his place of birth. This place on the margins makes it possible for Jesus to be claimed by those who live on the margins—that is, the shepherds. These are the people who have an intuitive sense of the mystery of life, seeing and hearing the angels among the stars. They will be the ones with eyes to notice a special baby among all the others in Bethlehem.

There is also a link between the words of the angels to the shepherds and the reign of Caesar Augustus. Augustus claimed to be the giver of peace to the empire. The Gospel writer is not making a political point, but rather is telling us that the only true peace can flow from this other way of looking at life, the life God offers, and it will flow from the child who will be found in Bethlehem.

 About the picture

The artist has followed the traditional convention of painting the nativity—a starry night, and a stable made of rough wood, with animals nearby. Later, Jesus will be taken to the temple and an offering of two turtledoves will be made to God in thanksgiving for his birth (Event 5). They are flying in the top corner of the picture. The great value of this picture is that it shows us Mary and Joseph together, with their newborn child. It is a very simple picture of family love, which matters far more than the odd place of the birth.

NB: The ox and the ass do not appear in either Gospel account, Matthew's or Luke's, and are simply part of a traditional retelling.

 Artist's eye

During the course of my research, I discovered that the birth of Jesus is one of the most painted images in Christian history, second only to Christ on the cross. This filled me with trepidation for two reasons. First, there was the challenge of tackling this scene in an original way so that it did not become a parody of greater and more established works of art; and second, I knew I would also have to paint Christ on the cross!

After much work, I eventually settled on quite a classical approach, showing the inside and outside of the stable. Inside are Mary, Joseph and the baby Jesus, with Joseph holding a teddy for the newborn child. Mary clutches the baby with mixed feelings—pride and fear of what the future has in store for her delicate and helpless infant. Outside are the classical symbols of the ox, the ass, and the two turtledoves that are later offered as a sacrifice.

 Looking at the picture

◈ Who is the artist telling us is the most important person in this picture? How can you tell this?

◈ What is the artist trying to tell us about the building in which Jesus was born?

◈ What time of day might it have been?

◈ What is he showing us at the top of the picture?

◈ How do you think Mary and Joseph must have felt at this moment?

◈ What makes this picture different from other pictures of the birth of Jesus that you have seen?

EVENT 3

The wise men

MATTHEW 2:1–12

The gifts have all been given symbolic significance, but it is not clear that Matthew intends anything more than the fact that they are expensive and are suitable gifts for a king.

The nativity story that is usually told at Christmas is a conflation of both Matthew and Luke's accounts, with added detail that has grown in the telling. While this is not wrong, it is important to recognize that each original writer, writing from a different part of the ancient Near East, began with a distinct viewpoint, and this is reflected in the material that they use. This material may again reflect the different sources that were available to them.

 About the picture

Sometimes Jesus is shown in pictures as an older child by the time the magi arrive, and that might be what is being shown here. The three men are correctly shown as travellers. The night sky and their guiding star form the background. Joseph is not present, and apart from his presence when Jesus is presented at the temple (Event 5) and the visit to the temple in Jesus' later childhood, we hear nothing more of him.

 Artist's eye

Three wise men come in search of the newborn king, bearing gifts of gold, frankincense and myrrh. They were probably physicians, fortune tellers, water diviners or astronomers. In any case, they were the holders of special powers or knowledge that separated them from the mainstream of society. The suggestion that they came from the east is the reason why they have unusual hats and highly decorated costumes.

Herod asks the men to send back news of the new king so that he too can honour the child. In fact, he wishes to dispose of Jesus, as he sees him as a threat to his authority.

The wise men follow the star of Bethlehem until they find the baby and, under a starry night sky, they deliver their gifts—but they do not return any messages to Herod. The night sky is actually a star constellation—I forget which one I used (I think it may have been the Seven Sisters or something similar).

 Background

The visitors from the east are recorded in Matthew's account of the nativity. In a similar place, Luke tells us that shepherds visited the child in the stable (Luke 2:1–20). In contrast to Luke, Matthew was interested in underlining the worldwide significance of Jesus' birth, so representatives of far-flung nations visit the baby. Matthew also wants to show that while some people accept Jesus' birth and worship him, others (for example, Herod) do not do so, and even turn to persecution. This way of looking at life will not be easy, and that was the continuing experience of the church for which Matthew wrote his Gospel.

The word that Matthew uses for wise men is *magi*, and it is likely that he means astrologers, although the word could mean 'magicians'. (Their traditional description as 'kings' is a much later addition, and not Matthew's intention.) There is no indication of the number of wise men—only that they give three gifts. Nor are we are given any clue about where they come from. 'From the east' may suggest Persia (modern Iran), but it is more important to Matthew that the wise men are non-Jews (Gentiles). When Matthew wrote his Gospel, Christians were coming to terms with the admission of Gentiles to what had been a predominantly Jewish church. What matters here is not who we are, but whether we are ready to 'see' things in this new and different way.

 Looking at the picture

◈ Why do you think the artist gives both Mary and Jesus a halo in this picture?

◈ How can you tell that the men are travellers?

◈ Can you tell which present is the gold, the frankincense or the myrrh?

◈ Can you imagine Mary's feelings at this moment?

EVENT 4
The killing of the children
MATTHEW 2:16–18

 Background

Matthew's story of the birth of Jesus is full of contrasts. The star guides, and then there is confusion. There is rejoicing at the birth of Christ, and then weeping. Matthew tells the story of Jesus' birth in a way that will be recognizable to Jews of his time. There was a legend that at the birth of Moses, Pharaoh was warned that a future liberator of the Israelites had been born. Fearing the consequences, he ordered all male Israelite babies to be slaughtered. Moses' father, warned in a dream of the danger, escaped with Moses to safety. Matthew sees Jesus as a new Moses. Herod, like Pharaoh, is troubled by the possibility of a rival, so in a callous act of power he does away with a whole generation of children to protect his throne. Joseph escapes with Jesus and Mary to Egypt, from which Jesus will return to Israel, just as Moses returned with the people of Israel in the exodus.

Parallels like this were very important to Christians as they tried to understand the significance of Jesus and explain his message to others. It was an attempt to get under the surface of a story and uncover the purposes of God. In our own age, this account points to the random nature of human violence, which, sadly, has all-too-frequent parallels in many contemporary historical events. Alongside real human possibilities for advancement and good we constantly have to set our capacity for regression and cruelty. This is the continuing context in which the message of Jesus is uncovered. It asks those who grasp it to commit themselves uncompromisingly to peace.

 About the picture

The agony of the woman in the centre of the picture leaps out at us from first glance. Armed soldiers attack a defenceless mother and her child. Her mouth is open in a great soundless cry, which seems to echo off the building behind. In the mother's lap the child lies rigid with fear. Swords dominate the picture, dragging the eye up and down, across and round. We understand that what we see here is one small scene from a much larger tragedy, impossible to look at. There is a terrible irony in the way the soldiers' combat uniform echoes the leaves of the tree. Leaves are a sign of life; the soldiers are destroyers of life. A grey bird with a fearsome red eye hovers like a malign spirit over the scene.

 Artist's eye

Herod, failing to hear any news from the wise men, is enraged. Fearing that his authority will be undermined, he sends out his troops to deal with this perceived threat. The troops are instructed to murder all baby boys under the age of two years.

I was particularly interested in how troops sent to cities still always wear their combat fatigues, as if they were in the jungle. In the urban landscape they stick out like sore thumbs, while in suburban and country areas their uniforms are better suited.

In this painting, surrounded by Herod's troops, a mother wails at the pointless death of her baby boy, who is cradled in her arms. The image of the wailing woman is influenced by Picasso's Guernica.

Herod is remembered in history as the patriarch who panicked at the so-called threat to his leadership and, in one moment of stupidity, sent out orders that would blight his name for eternity.

 Looking at the picture

◆ What is happening?

◆ How does the artist manage to convey this really terrible event?

If a copy of Picasso's *Guernica* is available, it would be useful to show it and discuss the reasons for its painting.

EVENT 5

Simeon praises the Lord

LUKE 2:22–35

 Background

This scene comes from Luke's Gospel, where it acts as a kind of bridge between the stories of Israel and the story of Jesus. Simeon and Anna (who does not appear in the picture but is an important part of the narrative) are recognizable figures from the history of Israel. Old and wise, they would have shared the common longing for Jerusalem and the Jewish people to be free of Roman rule. Jewish independence had come to an end 63 years earlier, when the Roman general Pompey marched on Jerusalem. He entered the temple, which was famed for its size and lavish decoration, and, out of curiosity, even went into the holy of holies—forbidden to all but the high priest. This was a scandal that had not been forgotten.

Luke uses strong imagery of light and darkness in this account. He is setting the scene for what is to come. Simeon 'sees', picking Jesus out from the many hundreds of babies he must have seen going in and out of the temple. He speaks of Jesus as a 'light for all nations'—that is, for Jews and for all people throughout the world. The possibilities opened by this child and this new way of looking at life are immense, but it will not necessarily be easy. He warns

Mary that she will suffer as though she had been 'stabbed by a dagger'.

The rite of purification was required of women 40 days after the birth of a child. Jewish law required that two young pigeons were offered to God at this visit.

 About the picture

A slightly startled Mary and Joseph stand in front of Simeon, who holds Jesus as he breaks into song. Joseph holds the bag of baby-changing equipment that all parents carry about when they go on a journey with a newborn baby. Mary holds Jesus' favourite toy. Overhead the light traps them all in its blaze, and Jesus stands out in his white shawl. The two turtle doves fly around— given to God, they are actually free. There is a sense of surprise, of the unexpected, like a light switched on suddenly to reveal something wonderful, but at the same time not fully understood.

 Artist's eye

Simeon has waited many years for this day. He is described as very old, with a grey beard. For Mary and Joseph this is a special event and they dress up in their finest clothes, as if to visit an important person. They also take along the essentials, such as a changing bag and favourite toy.

Simeon greets them in the temple with a huge sense of relief and happiness. He holds the baby and, in doing so, fulfils his mission to meet God's chosen deliverer before dying in peace.

In traditional paintings of this scene, the lighting comes from candles or a candelabra. I decided that it would be more contemporary to light the scene from above with an electric light bulb—again influenced by Picasso.

 Looking at the picture

◈ Can you describe what is going on in this picture?

◈ What atmosphere is the artist trying to convey?

◈ What clue do we have in the picture to show the importance of this particular baby?

◈ How do you think a mother and father feel when people admire their new baby?

EVENT 6
The boy Jesus in the temple
LUKE 2:41–52

Background

This story comes from Luke's Gospel, and is the last of his connecting stories between the faith of Israel and the teaching of Jesus. It was the custom for devout Jewish families to make an annual pilgrimage to the temple. This was often done in a large group, so there is nothing odd about Jesus not being noticed for a day. In fact, the point at which children began to take on responsibility for their actions was round about twelve. So Jesus, like other twelve-year-olds, would be allowed more freedom from his parents—but it was within limits, and Jesus' decision to stay in Jerusalem and talk with the doctors of the law in the temple clearly breaks the limits and hurts his parents.

Luke wants us to notice the play on the word 'father'. Who is Jesus' father? At this moment we are to see that Jesus is developing a strong sense of his relationship with God, and it is beginning to matter more than his relationship with Mary and Joseph. The ways diverge, and they do so with a familiar contrast of adolescent impatience and parental concern. Perhaps this is the beginning of the 'dagger' piercing Mary's heart that Simeon spoke of (Event 5). But in the end Jesus is obedient, and returns to Nazareth with them. We hear nothing more of him until his baptism by his cousin John.

In his Gospel, Luke weaves accounts of Jesus' childhood with those of John. The latter do not form part of this series, but can be found in the first two chapters of Luke.

About the picture

Jesus is the centre of the picture and the centre of everything that is happening in the story. On either side of him are the wise old men of Israel. They sit in the temple and talk. The book indicates that they are talking about Israel's history, which holds within it the Jewish understanding of God. The crook is a sign of authority: this is a chief priest, and someone of great importance.

Jesus is holding prayer beads. (These would not be part of a Jewish tradition: the artist is using some licence here.) He is young, but he prays deeply and as a result is able to talk with these wise men on an equal footing. They are amazed. Above them a light shines, and the spirit hovers watchfully. By contrast, Mary stands. She is impatient, clearly having just arrived, holding the water bottle that would have been necessary for a long journey in the sun. Jesus may be in a position of honour, but he has also broken the rules and she is anxious.

In front of them all, a chicken pecks at some seeds spilled from a bowl. The temple was also a place of buying and selling, because people brought animals to be given to God. As an adult, Jesus will return to the temple and clear out the stalls of the people who made profits from this trade, spilling birds and grain everywhere. He wanted the temple simply to be the house of God, which is how he experiences it here.

Artist's eye

Details about the life of Christ after his family's flight to Egypt to escape Herod's troops are few and far between. The only story in the Bible tells how he and his family go to Jerusalem to celebrate Passover. As they are travelling home to Nazareth, Mary and Joseph discover that the twelve-year-old Jesus is missing, so they return to Jerusalem. They find Jesus in the temple, sitting in discussion with the rabbi and the elders, who are impressed by his maturity and understanding.

Once more, the scene is lit from above and Jesus sits on a bench surrounded by the men of wisdom. They listen, protest and argue with the young Jesus. None of them notices Mary arriving on the scene after completing her long and worried journey back to find her lost son. They are too immersed in discussion with each other.

In the scene, a chicken runs around in the foreground, feeding on the grain scattered on the tiled floor. These symbols are a precursor to the time when Jesus revisits the temple as an adult and upturns the benches of the traders and money lenders in his protest at their abuse of his father's house.

Looking at the picture

◈ What is happening?

◈ Look at the faces of the three men. What is the artist trying to tell us about them? What are they thinking? What are they holding?

◈ Look at Jesus. What does he have in his hands? What does this suggest?

◈ In what way has the artist painted the figure of Mary differently from the others in the picture?

◈ Why has the artist chosen to include a lamp and a dove?

The story of Jesus (Part Two)

EVENT 7
The baptism of Jesus
Matthew 3:13–17

Background

In Mark's Gospel, the story of Jesus' life begins with this event of his baptism (Mark 1:9–11), but in Matthew we have already heard of the birth of Jesus, and already know something of who he is. There has been a long period of silence, during which Jesus is presumably working in Nazareth as a carpenter, like Joseph. Now he comes to his cousin John to be baptized.

John was scandalized by the corruption of contemporary religion and society. His stern message appears to have found a hearing, and people flocked to be baptized in the Jordan, promising to lead new lives. The place of the baptism, in the Jordan near Jericho, was powerfully symbolic, and Matthew inserts other images. Physically Jordan marked a boundary. On one side the land was fertile and cultivated. On the other it quickly gave way to wilderness. Here the Israelites crossed into the promised land after 40 years in the desert. It was a place of answers to promises and new beginnings.

Baptism was by immersion. Here again we are asked to see below the surface of things. Water washes, but baptism offers something deeper—an inner washing, making people ready to begin a new life. In the background to this is the story of the Israelites crossing another stretch of water—the Red Sea (Sea of Reeds)—leaving behind a life of slavery, to become free.

This whole scene continually asks us to open our eyes to the mystery that presses in. The dove of the Spirit hovers above and the voice of God is heard. This echoes the opening chapter of Genesis, where the Spirit of God broods on the face of the water, and God's word brings life to the world. Matthew wants his readers to understand that the Spirit of God is working again, offering the new and unexpected.

About the picture

Jesus stands up to his waist in the water, and the fish swim about his legs. In his sarong he looks vulnerable, waiting for John to pour the water. Above him is the strong white image of the dove. It is both in and out of the picture—part of what is beyond, but also very much present. Below the dove, the triangle of water flows to the centre. The river is alive with fish, and the water looks clear and inviting. There is something fresh, new and alive here. The trees on the banks flourish with their bright green leaves.

John leans over to pour the water. By contrast with Jesus, he is wrapped up, perhaps to protect him from the harsh sun of the desert. Near him is a locust, and round the edge of the picture is a pattern of honeycombs—desert food on which the tough John survives. We are at a moment of suspense, just before something very important is about to happen.

Artist's eye

According to Christian tradition, at baptism a person should be immersed in water three times. To achieve this with full immersion, one needs to be dipped backwards while standing shoulder-high in water.

For Jesus' baptism, I rejected this method because it looked too much like two men trying to drown each other. Instead, I have chosen a classical image based on the work of Pierro della Francesca, but showing a jug of water as a contemporary implement to carry out the baptism. Around Jesus' legs, fish swim in the living River Jordan.

John the Baptist is reported to have lived very frugally in the desert, surviving on a diet of locusts and wild honey, hence the locust at the bottom left and the honeycomb around the edge of the painting.

Looking at the picture

◈ What sort of place is the artist painting here?

◈ Do you think it might be a good place to be?

◈ What is the difference between the two men?

◈ What is happening between them?

◈ Why did the artist put an insect into the picture?

41

EVENT 8
The temptations of Jesus
MATTHEW 4:1–11

Background

We know nothing of Jesus' life from his infancy to his baptism by John in the Jordan (Event 7). The baptism marks the beginning of Jesus' ministry, a commissioning for the work God asks him to do. The Gospel writers tell us that 'straight away' after his baptism Jesus went into the desert. (The River Jordan marks a boundary between the settled land of Judea and the desert.)

The question Jesus faces in the desert follows on from the baptism, and centres round *what* his mission might be, and *how* he might fulfil it. He recognizes that he possesses considerable personal authority, but in what ways could it be used? To ensure, once and for all, that human hunger is satisfied? To reform the established religious systems of his day, and ensure that they are authentic? Or simply by the use of military power, which, once his authority had been established, could be used to usher in a world of lasting justice and peace? The point to grasp is that all these aspirations are good, but all require some kind of compromise to achieve their ends, and the compromise will, in the end, undermine the good results.

Good ends by doubtful means—hence the appearance of the devil. The devil in the Bible is often seen more as a lawyer, sifting out our motives, than as a personification of evil. The implicit choice here is for a way of life that responds to God's love for people and allows that love to dictate every action.

About the picture

The desert is shown by the rough mountains and large stones. In the distance is a Cornish tin mine (see the 'Artist's eye' notes below). Below it would be a maze of passages, perhaps symbolizing the way our minds burrow deeply into problems when we try to think things through. Jesus holds a carrier for water, and wears the sign of a fish around his neck, later used as a symbol for the church. The devil, pretending to be a farmer, has razor-sharp weapons: his method is sharp arguments and needling questions. His red eyes suggest danger. Above hovers a bird—perhaps a bird of the desert, but also perhaps the continuing watchful presence of the Holy Spirit.

Artist's eye

In an attempt to turn him away from his mission, the devil tempts Jesus after he has spent 40 days and nights in the desert. During this period, Jesus has to make do without food (but not water—hence the water bag he carries). Jesus is challenged to turn rocks into bread, jump from the highest part of the temple to prove that

he is the Son of God and, lastly, to gain the whole world in exchange for worshipping the devil. To each challenge, Jesus refuses.

While I was working on this painting, I visited St Ives in the west of Cornwall. On a tour of local galleries I saw a painting that handled a stone wall in an interesting way. I borrowed this for the top of the wall on which the devil stands. One painting of the scene that I saw shows many cities of the world behind the two figures, echoing the third temptation. This inspired me to include a silhouette of a Cornish tin mine. The west of Cornwall—one of my favourite places—is littered with abandoned tin mines. There is a saying in Cornwall that, wherever you go in the world, if you find a hole, at the bottom of it you will find a Cornishman. The devil holds a scythe, pretending to be a farmer to make his approach to Jesus. He is bedecked in lavish clothes and his red eyes betray his true identity.

Looking at the picture

◈ What kind of countryside is shown by the mountains and rocks?

◈ Why might the desert be a good place to go to, to think about something important?

◈ Look at the two people and see if you can see the difference between them.

◈ What might warn you that the man on the left is dangerous?

◈ What is the artist trying to tell us about the conversation between those two people?

◈ If you had to think through what to do with your life, where would you go?

EVENT 9

Jesus chooses his first disciples

LUKE 5:1–11

Background

In Luke's Gospel (it is not quite the same in Mark's account), Jesus has been teaching people alone for a while. Now it is as if he moves from the large crowd to draw together a small group of closer followers, who would be known as 'disciples'. The word means 'committed followers of a teacher'.

It was not uncommon at the time for a rabbi to have a small group of such followers who followed his teaching closely, but the way Simon Peter and his partners are asked is unexpected and surprising. They have been out all night fishing and have caught nothing. Night fishing was common practice: it was the time when the fish rose to the surface. By day the sun was too bright. After teaching the crowd about God, Jesus suggests that they go fishing. Peter protests but eventually agrees, and, out in the middle of the lake, the catch is enormous. This startles Peter and his friends. Nothing in their experience prepares them for it. The reason lies in Jesus and not in their skills, and they know it. It is as if an entirely new and unexpected life has broken into their lives. Luke's account tells us that there, in the boat in the middle of the lake (both oddly and dangerously!), they kneel down in surprise and awe. Jesus then asks them to leave everything and follow him.

The disciples are sometimes depicted as poor Galilean peasants, but in fact fishermen had a prosperous trade. The decision to follow Jesus meant giving up a comfortable home and a relatively secure way of life—and, given this huge catch, the possibility of some immediate and profitable trade. But the three men leave everything to take up the wandering life that Jesus lived, where they would depend for food and shelter on whatever they were given. So the story moves from a tale about ordinary fishermen to a story about people who have had a glimpse of a different way of life, lived out of the generosity of God. Their job will be to waken other people to this way of living.

About the picture

The boat rocks dangerously and one end of it seems to be sinking below the surface of the water as the two fishermen begin to pull on the heavy net. One stares at the huge catch of fish in disbelief while the other turns to Jesus, open-mouthed in amazement. Jesus holds the gaff, ready to help pull the catch on board. But there is no sense of danger here. In fact, the colours of the picture are bright, as if at this moment the light is very bright, showing everything up in transparent colour. This is an amazing, startling moment, one that the two men will never forget. They are skilled fishermen, but they have never known anything like this before. Jesus has changed everything.

Artist's eye

The part of the passage I chose to work on has, for me, the most action.

I could see Jesus out on the lake, with Peter and Paul in their sou'-westers, hauling in their bulging nets. The stern of the boat starts to settle as the weight of the fish increases. Jesus pulls at the nets with a boathook. Behind them flies the international flag signal for 'I am hauling nets'.

Painting the fish and the nets was the hardest part. Fishing nets are made from a line that is transparent in the water. In order to achieve this, the details of the net went in last, in watercolour, after all the fish and the side of the boat had been painted. There would be no second chances with this, as, if it went wrong, the watercolour would tarnish the colours underneath even if I tried to remove it. Any mistake would mean starting again.

Looking at the picture

◈ What is the first thing you notice?

◈ Look at the two ends of the boat. What is happening?

◈ What do you think the disciple who turns to Jesus is saying?

◈ What about the colours, compared to the other pictures? What is the artist trying to tell us?

◈ If you were a fisherman and you had just caught more fish than you had ever caught before, just because a man (who was not a fisherman) had suggested you go fishing, what would you think? What would you say?

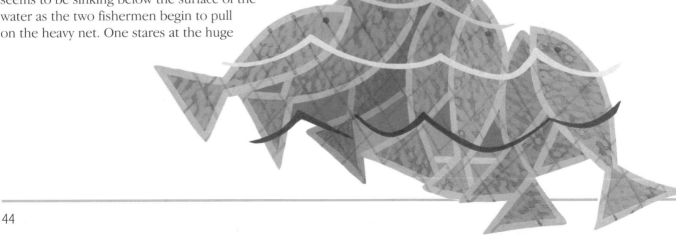

EVENT 10

Jesus heals a man

MATTHEW 8:1–4

 Background

This story, of a man being healed from a skin disease, is recounted by Mark (1:40–45), Matthew and Luke (5:2–16). The ancient world had an understanding of medicine, though it was limited. In addition, the Jewish law had some important rules for protecting society from contagious diseases.

Matthew describes the man's illness as leprosy, but the other writers describe it simply as a skin disease. At all events, a sufferer would be labelled 'unclean' and instructed to stay out of the community until the contagion had passed. In the case of a long-lasting disease, this could lead to great emotional and psychological suffering. Such unexplained illness terrified people and fed into a view of the world in which they saw themselves as the victims of random evil forces.

The man has no doubt that Jesus can help him: he says so straight out. He seems desperate. It was startling for Jesus to reach out and touch this man, both to the man and the surrounding crowds. The Gospel writers show Jesus as completely fearless in the face of illness, acting spontaneously out of great compassion for people. Whatever we think today about miracles such as this, the fact remains that the Gospels record a large number of incidents like this happening around Jesus. Jesus' own response seems to have been to play down these events, constantly telling those he healed not to tell others, even moving on when the crowds demanded more such miracles. His concern was that people should listen to his teaching, and not see him just as a wonder worker.

The story also shows that Jesus was loyal to the Jewish law. He tells the man to make the offering described in Leviticus, and to be officially certified as clean.

 About the picture

The artist captures the moment of intimacy when Jesus touches this isolated man. He is covered in bandages to prevent his sores from being more contagious than they are already. He carries a bell, which would warn people of his approach so that they could take avoiding action. Although one woman registers shock at the sight of someone unclean being touched, the crowds behind Jesus cheer at this man's return to society. Their pleasure suggests that they are cheering at more than the man's healing. A healer like Jesus would mean hope for them too if they were ill.

At the leper's side is a bowl. He would have been required, among other things, to give a quantity of flour to the priest when he went to be certified as clean, before he was fully returned to society.

 Artist's eye

It took two finished paintings to get this one right. In the first one, only Jesus and the leper were included. With hindsight, I came to the conclusion that this episode would have been far more public. In the final version of the painting, Jesus actually touches the leper. Those around him are struck with horror, made worse by the fact that the healing takes place on the Sabbath. A woman covers her mouth to stifle a scream, while a man in the background celebrates the miracle.

The leper, covered in bandages, has cast aside the bell that he is required to carry and Jesus touches him on the shoulder. Beside the leper is a bowl of olive oil and flour that he must offer to the priest, as confirmation that he is clean and can return to the mainstream of society.

 Looking at the picture

◈ What do you see happening?

◈ Why would someone be covered in bandages?

◈ What is Jesus doing?

◈ Do the people standing behind Jesus give us a clue about how people might feel when someone like this is healed?

◈ What would this make you think about Jesus?

EVENT 11

Jesus calms a storm

LUKE 8:22–25

 Background

Jesus spent much of his three years of ministry travelling around Palestine. This incident records a journey across Lake Galilee. The disciples are in a boat with him when a sudden storm blows up. Galilee is a landlocked lake, and the winds, trapped by the surrounding mountains, can quickly build up into a powerful force. Jesus sleeps. In contrast, the disciples in the boat are terrified. To people of the ancient world, this storm would not have been a natural phenomenon, but a manifestation of the power of demons. Hence Jesus *rebukes* these, to us, impersonal forces, and they *obey* him.

Again, the story points beyond itself to suggest the extraordinary nature of Jesus. He is more than just a great teacher or even a faith healer. Readers, like the disciples at this point, would ask, 'Who is this man, who can do these extraordinary things?' No answer is given here. It is another piece of the evidence that keeps us guessing.

 About the picture

The boat rocks in a terrifying way, threatening to tip the passengers into the stormy water. A bottle floats past, suggesting the desperation of someone shipwrecked on a deserted island. One oar is lost; the other does not engage with the water. The people in the boat are helpless, and they show signs of panic and terror. One man holds a red distress flare, poised to signal for help. Above them, the flag signals an emergency message. They are in deep trouble.

Meanwhile Jesus sleeps on. He is the picture of calm, unaware of the trouble going on around him. It is a sign of the disciples' panic that, up to now, they have not even noticed him!

 Artist's eye

I enjoyed painting this scene tremendously. Coming from a seafaring background, I am well acquainted with the sense of total helplessness someone might feel when at the mercy of the sea. The three disciples are in a state of absolute panic, fearing that they are about to drown, while Jesus dozes contentedly in a corner of the boat.

All attempts to control the boat have been abandoned as the oars jump from their rowlocks. The flag 'in need of assistance' has been hoisted as a signal to other vessels and one man lets off a red distress flare. The boat rears up uncontrollably and the waves claw the sides.

What struck me about this passage is that, even at this stage, the disciples still don't really understand who Jesus is. They know that he is someone important, but their amazement at how he commands the wind and waves underscores the fact that they have not yet reached the point at which they appreciate the magnitude of what they are involved in.

 Looking at the picture

◈ What is the scene that the artist is painting here?

◈ How can you tell that the disciples are frightened?

◈ Why did the artist include an empty bottle?

◈ What would you feel like in these circumstances?

◈ What might happen next?

EVENT 12
Jesus feeds five thousand
MATTHEW 14:13–21

 Background

Jesus withdraws after he hears of the death of his cousin John, but the crowds follow. Matthew notes that Jesus had compassion on them—translated as 'felt sorry' in the version printed here. 'Compassion' is a frequent word in the Gospels, implying that Jesus is motivated from within by a deep love for people, which must find expression in teaching and healing.

This miracle is recorded in all the Gospels, and John (6:1–13) adds the detail of the boy who comes forward with the loaves and the fish. Very quickly the story came to be associated by Christians with the sacrament of Holy Communion, a link that is made explicit in John's Gospel. It is clear that Matthew has a number of other ideas in his mind as he writes this account. The desert and the feeding with bread recall Moses in the wilderness and people finding 'manna', which was the dried white sap of a desert tree and resembled bread.

It is possible that the large crowds of people followed Jesus into the desert to rally to him now that John was dead. Perhaps they hoped that he would lead an uprising (Matthew's explicit reference to a count of men, rather than women and children, may imply this). Such a leader coming out of the desert was a contemporary expectation, but Jesus does nothing to encourage that expectation.

The miracle itself has no obvious explanation. It is sometimes suggested that the blessing of this small amount of food encouraged people to dig into their pockets and share the food they had brought—so the miracle becomes a miracle of sharing in the face of our usual selfishness. Perhaps—but Matthew seems to want to say that Jesus' teaching and presence are deeply satisfying to people: even a small encounter changes attitudes and helps people to live better lives. Jesus, for his part, had come looking for solitude to pray. Afterwards he sends the crowds and his disciples away and retreats into the wilderness.

 About the picture

Jesus stands at the end of the boat and holds the bread high. It glows in the evening light. Perhaps the artist is showing us that everything Jesus says and does is charged with a particular power, beyond our understanding, but real nevertheless. Already one member of the crowd seems to have a small piece of bread in his hand. A sack containing more bread stands beside the boat. Behind the crowd is the dry surface of the desert place. Later Jesus will send the crowd and the disciples away and retreat into this wilderness. This meeting with him in a strange place perhaps reminds us of unexplained events in our lives, after which we have felt better—though we find it hard to explain why.

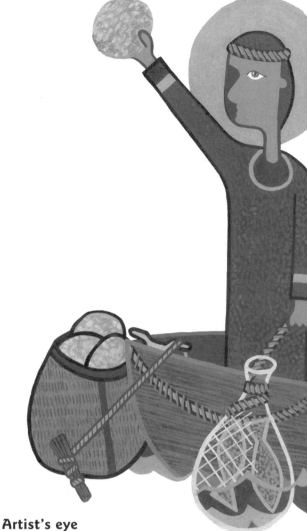

 Artist's eye

Jesus, saddened by the murder of John the Baptist, seeks solace and travels across Lake Galilee to be alone. However, as with any celebrity, his followers find out where he is. Touched by their loyalty and concerned for their comfort, he instructs his disciples to feed them. When it is discovered that there is very little food—only two fishes and five loaves—Jesus, still in his boat, raises a piece of bread to heaven for blessing. In a net at the side of the boat are two fish and, by the bow cleat, a sack of bread.

In many ways, this picture represents the ideal that society should be equal—everyone in the story is fed—an aspiration that still today we find hard to live up to.

Looking at the picture

◈ What do you think is the central point of this picture?

◈ What is everyone looking at?

◈ Can we tell what sort of place it is from the background?

◈ What time of day is it?

◈ If you were in a desert place with a lot of other people, and had only a small amount of food, what would you do?

EVENT 13

The true glory of Jesus

LUKE 9:28–36

Background

Jesus takes three of his disciples up a mountain and there, while he is at prayer, his robes take on the whiteness that is associated with divine reality. Standing with him are Moses and Elijah. These two men represent the different traditions of Jewish faith—the Law as given by Moses, and the Prophets of whom Elijah is the great example. They are also the two people in the Jewish tradition who experience God in the mystery of prayer on a lonely mountain top (Mount Sinai). For both of them, prayer has brought a profound encounter with God. The vision ends with the voice of God affirming Jesus once more.

This incident follows on from Jesus' attempts to explain the possibility of his future suffering to his disciples. They cannot understand. Now they have to hold together the idea of that possibly disastrous end to Jesus' life, and this new understanding of him as someone profoundly close to God. Peter wants to hold on to this experience: the 'shelters' would have been the booths that were erected in the fields at the time of harvest celebrations. It is not possible, though. From now on they have to work out the meaning as they follow Jesus.

About the picture

The figure of Jesus is striking. His robes are white, and behind him the clouds hint at the mystery of God. There is no mistaking the fact that he has an extraordinary power and authority. Beside him, Moses carries his staff as leader of Israel, and holds out a hand that had once been struck with leprosy. Elijah still carries the bread he begged from a woman. Both are framed, other-worldly, out of the past. Jesus by contrast has his feet firmly on this earth. In front, the disciples exhibit complete bewilderment. One sleeps; one stumbles upwards; Peter kneels, amazed at what he sees and hears.

Artist's eye

Jesus takes Peter, James and John out into the country to pray. The three disciples fall asleep, presumably tired after the long journey, and Jesus goes on praying by himself. The three are awoken by a blinding light to find Jesus talking to the two Old Testament figures, Elijah and Moses. Elijah and Moses represent the cornerstones of the traditions of Israel and this meeting fulfils the prophecy of the Old Testament concerning the coming saviour.

The disciples have mixed reactions: one is still asleep, one is just waking up and is startled, and only Peter, Jesus' most loyal disciple, has some inkling of what is going on.

Moses has bare feet, as a reference to his encounter with the burning bush. His hand is highlighted, recalling the time when he placed his hand inside his shirt and pulled it out to find that it had turned white as snow. Elijah holds a piece of bread as a reference to the time when he sought bread from a woman. Both are inside their own frame, as if they are in the doorway to another world.

Jesus shines and his clothes glow, while behind him are the cloud formations that represent God.

This event is significant in that it occurs at the time when the disciples, particularly Peter, finally begin to understand who Jesus is. Now, when it is almost too late, they are becoming aware of the magnitude of the events that are, and will be, taking place.

Looking at the picture

◈ What would a white robe mean in a painting like this?

◈ What is the artist trying to say by putting the two men on the left in a frame?

◈ Look at the disciples in front. Can you tell what they are thinking?

The story of Holy Week and Easter

EVENT 14
Jesus enters Jerusalem
MATTHEW 21:1–11

Background

Jesus has been slowly walking towards Jerusalem with his disciples. They still do not understand what he has to tell them about the way this journey will end. When they arrive in Jerusalem, the crowds turn out to shout and cheer, and this must have added to the disciples' confusion. The arrival of someone with Jesus' personal authority and reputation in the holy city of Jerusalem was bound to encourage people's hopes. Some would have remembered a prophecy in Zechariah (9:9), which referred to a king arriving on a donkey. It was also very near the feast of the Passover. Jerusalem would be crowded and national feeling would be high. The Passover celebrated liberation from slavery in Egypt and its prayers specifically looked to the coming of the future leader—the Messiah. The Romans always feared trouble at Passover time and the garrison would have been strengthened.

Although Matthew describes this entry in almost regal terms, there is also an air of mystery. How does the donkey owner know to give them his animal? The point being made in Zechariah is about a humble king, not someone who is going to lead an army against the Romans. People cheer, but the message Jesus conveys is not the one they are expecting. It is after this that Jesus goes into the temple and clears out the traders. Again, this is not the act of someone who is going to be a nationalistic leader.

Jesus looked for a purifying of this sacred house of prayer, and the purpose of his preaching was to draw people back to a true relationship with God. The issue of Roman occupation was not what concerned him. But inevitably Jesus' sheer goodness exposed the hypocrisy of the religious leaders. His words and actions were taken as an act of defiance by the chief priests, who sided with the Romans in their desire to avoid trouble.

About the picture

The road is covered with leaves and coats. There is a general air of rejoicing. The walls of Jerusalem look thick and strong, as if Jesus is going into a fortress. Jesus rides his donkey carefully. It is not a very dignified animal. We have to wonder if the crowds really understand who Jesus is and what he intends to do.

Artist's eye

Although the mention of two donkeys in the Gospel passage is very interesting, I decided to take the traditional approach to this story by showing Jesus on a single donkey, entering through the gates of Jerusalem. The crowd is gathered around him, with people laying down clothes on the ground. Above, a man is perched high in a tree, breaking off branches to pass down so that they too can be strewn under the donkey's feet. These are traditional symbols of the people of Jerusalem welcoming someone very important and special into their city. Jesus sits proudly on the donkey, accepting the adoration of the crowd.

Looking at the picture

◈ What are people doing in this picture?

◈ What atmosphere is the artist trying to show to us?

◈ Have you ever ridden a donkey? What does it feel like?

◈ Look at Jesus. What do you think is going through his mind?

EVENT 15

Jesus washes the feet of his disciples

JOHN 13:4–12

Background

In a society where people walked everywhere, barefoot or wearing sandals, it was customary for wealthy households to appoint a slave to wash their guests' feet at the door. It is this lowly task that Jesus carries out for his disciples, turning their relationship with him upside down. Teachers were deeply honoured by their followers and students. Such a reversal of what seemed a God-given order would have being shocking.

In his conversation with Peter, Jesus makes it clear that he is modelling a new way of living. Just as he serves Peter and washes his feet, so Peter must serve others. The obligations of hierarchy have gone, and in their place is the equality of friends. As the disciples serve and care for each other and extend this service beyond themselves to others, they will discover that God works through them to bring in the kingdom. The point being made here is that the love Jesus shows through this action changes people and creates a society that has the power to change things beyond itself. At this moment, Peter does not understand; after the resurrection, he will.

This account is found only in John's Gospel, and John has no account of the meal recorded by the other three Gospel writers. The only one in his account who eats something is Judas—and Judas goes out immediately afterwards to betray Jesus. But the foot washing and the meal both give the same message: the new community Jesus is creating must be one marked by the same quality of compassion and love that has marked his life. When people learn to live in this way, new worlds of understanding will be opened to them.

About the picture

All the eyes in the picture are turned to Jesus, who is on his knees, washing the feet of one of his disciples. Behind him, his robe is hung up. He has a towel around his waist. The disciples to the right are shocked, and hold up their hands in horror. They have agreed to have their feet washed, but the stiff pose of the disciple in the centre of the picture suggests that he is agreeing reluctantly. He does not yet understand.

To the left stands Judas, his eye red. Does this indicate anger at the final betrayal of the leadership that he had always hoped Jesus would show? He is marked off from the others now. They may not understand, but their loyalty to Jesus is complete. Judas can no longer be loyal: he is already imagining what he can do. Strangely, Jesus seems to see that. There is a visible shadow creeping across the picture. Jesus has no illusions about the consequences. Outside it is night.

Artist's eye

The washing of the disciples' feet during the Last Supper is recorded only in John's Gospel. According to the synoptic Gospels (Matthew, Mark and Luke), the meal itself took place around the time of the celebration of Passover. John, however, says that it occurs before Passover, based on the assumption that the crucifixion takes place on the day before Passover. This could, however, be a symbolic use of the timing to place the death of Jesus at the same time as the sacrifice of the paschal or Passover lambs.

For the purposes of this painting, I have combined all four Gospel accounts. The meal is a paschal or Passover meal, and the washing of the disciples' feet takes place during the preparation for the meal.

The disciples were shocked and confused by Jesus' actions when he knelt down and humbly began to wash their feet. Peter is particularly indignant and covers his mouth in horror. When Jesus points out the symbolism of the act, Peter asks to have his hands and head washed also. Jesus replies that he is already clean and, at this point, shows Judas that he knows he has planned to betray him. How this could be shown in a visual image posed a bit of a problem. Most versions of the foot washing simply show the humble act itself and do not depict how Judas plays a specific role in this event. I decided that the reference to one of the disciples being unclean would be a useful device to separate Judas from the rest, so he is shown as the only one still wearing his shoes. He is also partially in shadow.

Jesus kneels at the feet of one of the disciples and is surrounded by the pots and bowls that contain the herbs and lotions. Around his waist he wears a towel and in the background hangs the overgarment that he removed.

Looking at the picture

◈ Where do all the eyes in this picture lead?

◈ What is Jesus doing?

◈ What does he have round his waist?

◈ What is the artist trying to tell us about the attitude of the disciples on the right?

◈ Who is the disciple on the left?

◈ What is on his mind, and how is the artist telling us about what he is thinking?

◈ Look through the window. Is what it shows important?

EVENT 16
The Lord's Supper
MATTHEW 26:20–30

 Background

We have an account of the Lord's Supper in Paul's letter to the Corinthians (1 Corinthians 11:23–25), an account that was written a number of years before the first Gospel was written. Paul was giving instructions about the conduct of Christians at this meal, so it is clear that it has been part of Christian worship from the earliest times. While the meal is clearly associated with the Passover (Jesus is crucified just before the Passover festival), it cannot have been a Passover Seder. That would have happened on a Friday night—the day of Jesus' death. However, there can be no doubt that Jesus associated his death with the Passover, and this meal shares many Passover features—the hope that God will lead us into freedom and new life, and the establishing of a new covenant between God and us.

All meals are acts of sharing. We give something of ourselves when we sit round a table and share food. By breaking the bread and sharing the cup so deliberately, Jesus is modelling the generosity that has so marked his life—a giving away of himself. One possible translation of Jesus' words is, 'This is me, this is what I am like.' The purpose of his death will again be a giving away of his life, and he invites the disciples to live with the same generosity and compassion. 'Do this…' refers to both the meal, which they are to repeat, and his way of life, which it will remind them to follow. Peter still does not understand either himself or the way of life that Jesus has been trying to explain to him. In all the Gospels, he makes brave promises, only to go back on them later. It is only after the resurrection that he at last begins to understand fully.

 About the picture

The disciples gather round the table, at which they would have been reclining rather than sitting in chairs. Their shoes are removed, as was the custom. It is a solemn moment, and Jesus holds the cup high, as if he were using it to call on God. The hand gestures show that the disciples are aware that this is a most solemn moment. The cup and the bread are firmly in Jesus' hands—part of him. The remains of the meal are on the table, but the disciples' attention is focused on Jesus and his words.

Judas looks away; he has things on his mind. In front of Peter a cockerel hovers. Peter will make brave boasts, which Jesus knows he cannot carry out. By dawn the next morning when the cockerel crows, Peter will have gone back on his word and he will weep. Behind him on the wall is a patch of red, dripping. It was the Passover custom to paint a door with the blood of a lamb, to remind people of the day of escape from Egypt. Here it reminds us that for Jesus there will be no escape. Judas' red eye makes the connection.

 Artist's eye

If we work on the basis that this was at least a paschal meal, we can begin to pull in the details of a Passover or similar symbolic meal. The common assumption is that only bread and wine are served. However, a paschal meal is a proper feast with many courses and four symbolic cups of wine.

The bread that becomes the body of Christ is one of three pieces of unleavened bread, the middle piece of which is torn in half and one half of it wrapped in linen to eat as a dessert at the end of the meal.

The meal begins with symbolic hand washing (possibly derived from the foot washing) and eating of herbs dipped in vinegar to symbolize the oppression of the people of Israel before their exodus. The meal itself is historically the last one that the Jewish people ate before escaping the oppression of Egypt. It is ironic that Jesus escapes his own oppression as an infant by escaping to Egypt.

There are various dishes on the U-shaped table and the participants traditionally sit on the floor in a reclining position. In front of Peter, who is dumbfounded at Jesus' declaration that his own death is imminent, stands a cockerel indicating Jesus' assertion that Peter will deny Jesus three times before the cock crows. Behind Peter's head, blood is painted on the wall, indicating both the lamb's blood painted on the walls of the oppressed people of Israel, which the angel of death would pass over in the exodus, and the blood that Jesus spills on the cross.

When I first painted this bloodstain, I was unsure whether or not to leave it in. I had painted the Last Supper before the washing of the disciples' feet, and I wasn't sure how they would work together. However, when I finally saw the two paintings together, I was convinced that I had done the right thing to leave the bloodstain in. The contrast was appropriate. It conveys the humility of the foot washing followed by the significance of the Eucharist (the Lord's Supper).

Judas' heart races as he realizes that he has been calmly accused. He is alone with his thoughts, excluded from the rest of his former friends. Later, those who feel smug are quietly informed by Jesus that, although they are not betrayers, they will all deny their association with him in the hours ahead.

 Looking at the picture

◈ What is on the table?

◈ Look at the disciples' faces. Can you see one that is different? What is he thinking?

◈ Look at Jesus and then look at the three disciples' faces and hands.

◈ What is the artist telling us about their attitudes and feelings?

◈ Look at Jesus. What is he doing with the bread and the cup?

◈ Why is the cockerel there?

EVENT 17

Jesus is arrested

MATTHEW 26:47–56

 Background

It is very clear from the Gospels that Jesus was under no illusions that the authorities, whether religious or secular, were eager to get rid of him, so this moment of arrest was not a surprise. Jesus had also tried to warn his disciples that this outcome was inevitable, but they could not accept his analysis. What is less clear is the motivation of Judas. Perhaps he was a nationalist who was disappointed that Jesus had rejected the idea of political or military action. Perhaps he was a religious fanatic who thought that, by drawing this aggressive action on to a supremely good man, he could trigger a divine intervention. But that is not the concern of the Gospel writers. What interests them is that the shadow side of human nature has come to the surface, irrationally and destructively. Here in the garden, the shadow attempts to overwhelm the one person who seems to embody light and hope, namely Jesus.

Jesus' response is utterly consistent with his whole way of living and teaching. Violence is rejected: he does not resist. In Luke's account of this incident, he heals the wounded ear of the high priest's servant (Luke 22:51). From now on, it is as if Jesus digs ever more deeply into the source of love and compassion in himself to confront the darkness and destructiveness. Nothing will deflect him from this course.

 About the picture

The picture reflects the confusion of the moment, and is hard to read at first sight. The two key figures are at either side. Judas, clutching his bag of money in the top left, is not playing any part in the mayhem he has caused. Jesus is on the right, calm and unsurprised, holding out a hand to restrain Peter. He stands at the apex of a triangle, the pivotal figure in all of the action. In the centre, Peter attacks the high priest's servant, and the sliced ear lies on the ground. At the back, the soldiers emerge from the bushes, strongly armed to arrest a man who has no weapons. Across the lower portion of the picture lies a red shadow, hinting at the pain that is to come.

 Artist's eye

What really struck me about this episode was the absolute chaos that must have broken out immediately after the kiss from Judas. Soldiers appear out of nowhere. It is dark and confusing; there is noise and shouting. Peter slices the ear off one of the high priest's servants, who shrieks in agony and clutches the side of his head. Judas looks on, holding his bag of booty and wondering if his actions will reap the results that he hoped for. Jesus gestures to Peter to put his sword away.

Judas is an interesting character. I see him as a political figure, keen to see the end of Roman oppression. Perhaps he thought that, with Jesus in custody, the masses of followers would revolt to rescue Jesus and start a civil war.

 Looking at the picture

◈ Can you work out what is happening in this picture?

◈ What do you think the artist is telling us when he uses the colour red?

◈ Can you work out what Jesus might be saying to Peter?

◈ Look in the top corner. Who is this? What is he doing? What might he be thinking?

◈ Do you think it was necessary to use armed soldiers to arrest Jesus?

EVENT 18

Pilate questions Jesus

MATTHEW 27:11–26

Background

After his arrest, Jesus is taken before the Jewish court, the Sanhedrin. Various witnesses come forward who give a false account of things Jesus has said. The high priest finally challenges Jesus about his claim to be the Son of God. Jesus does not deny this claim, and he is condemned, but the Sanhedrin, although it would want to pass the death sentence for what would be regarded as blasphemy, has no power to do so. That rests with the Romans, so Jesus must be taken before Pilate, the Roman governor.

Pilate would be determined to avoid any possibility of trouble during the festival, but he also seems wary of the Sanhedrin's claims. This is reinforced by his wife's dream that Jesus is innocent. He resorts to a strategy which, if it worked, would bypass the Sanhedrin. His custom has been to release a prisoner at Passover time, and now he puts a choice to the crowd: Jesus who is called Christ, or Jesus Barabbas—a known criminal.

Pilate had clearly expected the crowd to choose Jesus of Nazareth, but, encouraged by the Sanhedrin, they choose Barabbas. Pilate's action in washing his hands has its origins in Jewish law, but is only permitted for those who have genuinely had no involvement in the death of an innocent person—something that Pilate could not really claim. So Jesus is condemned, and it becomes the responsibility of the Roman garrison to carry out the crucifixion. Scourging was the regular Roman practice before the execution of a criminal.

About the picture

Jesus is highlighted in the light of a bright lamp, like so many political prisoners. Ropes bind him tightly. On his head is a crown of thorns. He stands silently before Pilate, who is solemnly washing his hands. Behind Pilate, his wife whispers in his ear. But it is too late. Pilate has a fixed gaze. He has done what he could and it has failed, so now he has to go through with an unpleasant condemnation. Beside Jesus stands a soldier waiting for the next order. The procedure is not unfamiliar to him and he is ready for the next action. From his hands a long whip snakes across the floor. Outside there are spectators, rows of them, and the structure of the painting eventually brings our eyes to rest there, as if

we end up being part of the crowd. Above the crowd is a dark bird. It is a better place to be than in the room, but are these innocent bystanders?

Artist's eye

Jesus stands bound before the procurator of Judea, Pilate, who has the power to authorize the death of a prisoner. Pilate was probably in Jerusalem to oversee the Passover in case of any trouble, which is why he was right at the centre of the action. He was a political figure and held his position as a prefect for ten years or more, showing that he was quite successful as a regional governor. As a career politician, he tried to avoid really difficult decisions, such as what to do about Jesus, as a wrong turn might provoke a violent reaction and discredit him to his Roman superiors. So, in true political style, he defers the decision to others—the crowd gathered outside. It is highly likely that not all of the crowd were Jewish. There were probably Roman 'plants', other agitators, temple police and representatives whipping the crowd on and trying to influence events.

Jesus' fate is sealed. He wears the scarlet robe of a Roman officer and a crown of thorns tears into his forehead. Beside him stands a Roman soldier holding a whip, ready to inflict the second wound on the condemned Christ. Jesus has a spotlight angled into his face during this interrogation as, I suspect, today's political prisoners might, and Pilate symbolically washes his hands of the whole situation. His wife whispers in his ear.

In the frame of the window, the crowd jeers and cajoles Pilate into condemning Jesus. A crow flies overhead.

Looking at the picture

◈ What do you notice first?

◈ What are we being told about Jesus by the way he is painted?

◈ Can you guess why the man on the right is washing his hands?

◈ What is the woman on the right doing?

◈ Can you see through the window? What part are these people playing?

◈ Is there a hint of what might happen next?

EVENT 19

Jesus is nailed to a cross

MATTHEW 27:31–54

Background

Although the artist has painted a picture that shows the suffering of Jesus, the Gospel writers tend to dwell very little on this. They are more interested in what they see as the confrontation between the underlying brutality and evil that human nature is capable of—shown by this extraordinarily cruel form of torture and death and the power of love present in Jesus, which counters it. This conflict is played out like a great drama across the whole of the accounts of Jesus' trial, and it reaches its climax here on the cross.

Jesus says very little during the crucifixion. He asks for water, and is given vinegar—commonly given to help relieve pain. He also quotes from Psalm 22, a poem in which the depths of human loneliness and depression are explored: 'My God, my God, why have you deserted me?' He is silent in the face of cruelty. In Luke's account of this episode, Jesus even forgives the soldiers as they drive in the nails (Luke 23:34). Whatever is happening to him, his whole focus is on the love of God which, despite the dereliction, he believes ultimately has not deserted him, and never will. At this moment, Jesus trusts that goodness and love, rooted in God, is more powerful than the massed cruelty of human nature. The Gospels record that Jesus died at three o'clock, though it was not uncommon for victims of crucifixion to linger for days.

Matthew writes all this in graphic colours—an earthquake, darkness at noon, the curtain of the temple torn, the astonishment of the soldiers. The point is to underline the huge significance of this event, which must have taken place on a derelict hill of execution, from which everyone, including the disciples, stayed away. The only people to stay around are Jesus' mother, perhaps Mary of Magdala, another woman named Salome, and the disciple John.

Apart from the reference in Matthew to Joseph of Arimathea offering a tomb, the rest of the story of Joseph is legend. However, the link between the cross and Holy Communion is central to Christian tradition. Jesus shared the last supper 'on the night he was betrayed', fully aware of what was to happen to him the following day. The sacrament of Holy Communion encourages Christians to live with the same costly love.

About the picture

There is no mistaking the pain of the crucifixion here. Above the cross are the words that Jesus is recorded to have said during his three hours on the cross: 'My God, my God, why have you deserted me?' The soldier stands guard to prevent any rescue attempts. His hammer (see 'Artist's eye' notes below) did not need to be used on Jesus.

At the foot of the cross, Joseph of Arimathea fills a chalice. Blood represents life, so the symbolism here is that Jesus shares his life with those who follow him—hence the importance of the chalice, the shared cup of Holy Communion. John, who is one of Jesus' disciples, Mary, Jesus' mother, and his friend Mary Magdalene stand in horror at the foot of the cross. Darkness fills the sky and the red of pain ebbs about the bottom of the picture.

Artist's eye

Jesus receives his last three wounds—to his hands, his feet and his side. Painting this image was an extraordinarily emotional experience. This has been the most oft-painted Christian image in the last two thousand years. Some of the greatest image makers and talented artists were, and still are, challenged by this subject matter.

During the course of my research, I unearthed an image of Christ on the cross taken from a book about the quest for the holy grail—the vessel that Jesus used at the Last Supper. In this image, Joseph of Arimathea collects the spilt blood of Jesus in the grail and, in an instant, the grail becomes the most sought-after object in Christian history. This was a powerful and intriguing idea and one that I decided to use. Joseph of Arimathea diligently and furtively collects Jesus' blood as it trickles down his legs, and Jesus, his face turned to heaven, cries out to his father in Aramaic, 'My God, my God, why have you deserted me?'

In Rubens' famous painting of the event, we see a Roman soldier wielding a huge iron bar to break the legs of one of the thieves while the thief himself pulls his ankles away from the wooden cross and the nail passes right through his leg. Hence, in my painting, the Roman soldier stands with a hammer in his hand and spear at the ready to strike the final blow if need be. At the same time, I wanted to build in the account of the sky turning black and the Roman soldier realizing that Jesus must in fact be the Son of God. To the right, a crowd looks on aghast; the woman could be Jesus' mother with hands held to her face in disbelief. Other witnesses look on.

Looking at the picture

◈ Can you describe this scene?

◈ How does the artist tell us that this is a terrible event?

◈ Look at the cup, or chalice. What do we use these large, special cups for?

◈ Look at the people beside Jesus. What would your thoughts have been if you were there?

eli, eli, lama sabachthani ?

EVENT 20

Jesus is alive

MARK 16:1–8

 Background

The artist has taken his picture from Mark's Gospel, but he has altered it—understandably perhaps, though missing the careful detail of the original text. Mark's Gospel ends in a curious and, we now think, deliberate way. It is not Jesus that the women see at the tomb, but a young man who tells them that Jesus is risen and they will meet him in Galilee. (In fact, none of the Gospels, following Mark's account, have Jesus meeting the women at the entrance to the tomb. Angels guard the entrance and it is always elsewhere that Jesus appears.) But there is an odd problem with the text in Mark. It seems as if he ended his Gospel immediately afterwards, at verse 20, with the women going away afraid. There are some extra verses, but these appear to have been written by someone else at a later date. So, in fact, there is no resurrection appearance as such in Mark's text, only news of the resurrection.

It was once thought that the real ending of Mark had been lost over the time when the manuscript was being copied and recopied. Now we are not so sure. It would be consistent with the way Mark writes his Gospel to leave us with an open question. Those who read the story of Jesus in this book will believe, and discover Jesus risen in their own experience—or they will not. Mark does not force the matter. It is also interesting to note that, in all the Gospels, it is to the women that Jesus first appears. Salome appears to have been a disciple of Jesus. She is mentioned as being with the other women at Jesus' crucifixion in Mark 15:40–41 and, in some very early Christian manuscripts, she is described as a disciple of Jesus.

 About the picture

The dark hole of the tomb at the centre of this picture very quickly catches the eye. The dark reality of death is very close here. That is what has brought the women to the tomb, clutching at their spices to anoint the body. Arriving here, however, they find everything utterly changed. Sitting on the stone that once sealed the tomb is a figure depicted here as Jesus, alive with a life that seems to radiate from him. That it is the Jesus who has been crucified is evident from the marks of the nails in his ankles, but now he lives, unmistakably. The staff he holds is a sign of his authority under God. Opposite him, the women are overcome with a range of emotions—joy, astonishment and awe. The jars of spices are forgotten: one is even dropped in the surprise. Across the front of the picture a soldier sleeps. He misses everything. His sword and spear lie uselessly beside him.

 Artist's eye

Joseph of Arimathea is the character who arranges for the proper burial of Jesus' body. After the Sabbath, Mary Magdalene, Salome and the mother of James set off to anoint Jesus' body with herbs and lotions. They arrive to find the huge stone rolled away from the entrance to the tomb and a man in white robes.

The women are shocked to find the tomb open and a man waiting for them. They drop the herbs and sink to their knees. I decided that I would not use an angel or messenger, but Jesus himself—hence the blue robe that shows the wounds to his ankles. White does not reproduce well, so I have only given him a white outline.

There are several reasons why the tomb would not have been guarded. Perhaps, as in Matthew, an earthquake frightened the soldiers away, or perhaps they were asleep. Here, as the resurrected body of Jesus waits on the sealing stone, a soldier slumbers. In the background, the orange morning sun begins to rise.

 Looking at the picture

◈ What do you think the dark hole in the centre is, or was?

◈ Who is on the right? Is there any difference in the way he has been painted?

◈ What do you think the women on the left are thinking and feeling?

◈ Does the artist help us to understand this?

◈ Using the picture, can you retell the story of what has happened, including the soldier at the bottom?

EVENT 21
Jesus and Thomas
JOHN 20:24–29

Background

This scene comes at the end of John's Gospel. Jesus has already appeared to the disciples in the upper room, but on that occasion Thomas was not present. When they tell him who they have seen, Thomas is uncertain. How could someone who he knew had most certainly died now be alive? So Thomas holds out for concrete evidence.

A week later, Jesus appears again. He seems to come through closed doors. They may have been closed because of the disciples' fear of arrest, but this is also a way of telling the reader that Jesus, though recognizable, was not bound by his human body or, indeed, earthbound at all. Confronted by the recognizable scars, Thomas believes, with a phrase that sums up the whole of the gospel: 'You are my Lord and my God!'

The point John seems to be making here is that the reader, like Thomas at first, does not see the risen Jesus. Thomas, who throughout John's Gospel has always asked the questions that begin to clarify what is meant, sees and believes. It is entirely right to wonder and to question, and those who do so and who believe, even though they do not see, will be even more blessed in their eventual understanding than Thomas was.

About the picture

The pairing of Jesus and Thomas in the middle of the picture presents a curious scene. Jesus stands, open, vulnerable, ready to answer any questions that might be put to him. The wounds are there, and Thomas is reaching out to make sure that this really is the truth that stands before him. His hand, held to his mouth, tells us that it is. Around them both stand the disciples, awed, shocked and, in the case of the man on the left, delighted to have Jesus with them again. It is almost as if the hand is there to restrain Jesus and make him stay. On the floor lie the nails that once held Jesus to the cross—another piece of evidence for Thomas, if he needed it. Above, the Holy Spirit flies, comfortingly, as if guarding them from harm.

Artist's eye

After his death, Jesus appears to his disciples and others. Luke states that the testimony of the three women who first see the resurrected Jesus is an idle tale. In the other Gospels there is also some doubt about whether the disciples actually believe that Jesus has risen from the dead as he said that he would.

The story that I found most interesting is in John, where Thomas, a seldom-featured disciple, will not accept the concept of the resurrection without seeing it for himself. In a gathering of the disciples in a closed room, Thomas is confronted by Jesus. For pictorial purposes, Jesus is dressed as he was on the cross and his body shows the wounds of crucifixion still seeping blood. Thomas surveys the man before him and pokes his hand into the wound in Jesus' side, thus proving beyond doubt that this is no trick.

I recalled a poem by Roger McGough when I was reading this passage, about a child who answers the door to his house in 1970s Liverpool. During the course of events, the child and his mother, desperate to get rid of the 'crank' at the door, give a glass of water to the man, and the man gives the child three rusty nails. I carried this idea of the nails into the painting, so they are lying around on the floor, still stained with blood. I did this to show that, in spite of the miracles, the transfiguration and the events surrounding Jesus' death, Thomas and others still doubt the authenticity of the man before them. Had I witnessed for myself Jesus raising people from their graves, calming the elements and healing those with long-term illnesses, I suspect that I would not have been too surprised to see this person come back from the abyss.

Looking at the picture

◆ Can you tell what is happening here?

◆ What is the man to the right of Jesus thinking as he reaches out his hand?

◆ What do the other disciples think at this moment?

◆ How do you know that everyone has been surprised by Jesus' coming into the room?

◆ What else is in the picture?

EVENT 22
The coming of the Holy Spirit
ACTS 2:1–12

 Background

This account comes from the beginning of the second book Luke wrote in the New Testament—the Acts of the Apostles—which describes the life of the church, following on from the life of Jesus. The life of the church begins with an extraordinary event—the coming of the Holy Spirit. Luke's account is very careful in its precise descriptions. The day is the Jewish festival of Pentecost, a day on which Jews celebrate not only harvest, but the giving of the law to Moses on Mount Sinai. It was a day on which many people, scattered over the empire, would make a point of returning to Jerusalem to celebrate, so Jerusalem is crowded.

The event in the house where the disciples have gathered was so powerful an experience that Luke has to describe it in symbolic terms—wind and fire, and an individual commissioning of each disciple by a tongue of flame on each person's head. So invaded are they by this Spirit that each of the disciples begins to speak in languages they themselves evidently did not under-stand. The noise in the house is so loud that it spills out into the surrounding streets. The visitors to the city, overhearing what is spoken, claim to recognize their own languages coming, oddly enough, from a group of people who had rarely travelled beyond Galilee, let alone outside Palestine.

The experience of speaking in tongues, though not common, happens often enough to be a recognized response to a powerful, overwhelming sense of the presence of God. People speak in languages they do not themselves understand, but which can be understood by others in the group. Luke may be recounting such an experience, but by the time he has finished this story of the church, the message of Jesus has been spread far across the Roman Empire, to many of the places from which these languages come. So this experience foreshadows the story that the rest of the book will tell.

 About the picture

At the top of the picture, like an explosion, the Holy Spirit breaks through the arch of the ceiling into the room where the disciples are gathered. Great jagged tongues of flame bear down into the room, seeking each disciple and touching their heads and hearts. The disciples, including a child, stand amazed, though the disciple to the right is already beginning to speak. To the left, Peter, the acknowledged leader of the group, stands—his cross suggesting his office and the keys representing his authority to forgive and bless. His sword, wrongly used in the garden, is ready to be abandoned. To his right is Mary, mother of Jesus, who continues to have an important place among her son's disciples. A sack of oranges is to the right (see 'Artist's eye' notes below). At the front, the child, holding his toy, stares up at the Holy Spirit in amazement. Perhaps he stands for the next generation of Jesus' followers, who will find out for themselves what all this means.

 Artist's eye

The coming of the Holy Spirit occurs during the 'festival of weeks', a celebration of harvest that is a very important date in the Jewish calendar. Jews from many nations are gathered together in Jerusalem for the event.

In my painting, a dove, complete with halo and flames, represents the Holy Spirit. The two men at the right and left hear the message in their own language. A woman, possibly Mary, looks up in awe, as does a child clutching his toy train. Behind them is a sack of oranges. I have included this as a reference to the fact that modern Israel is quite famous for its Jaffa oranges and Jaffa was an important port even in Jesus' time.

Peter is restored to a position of leadership, despite his denials. His sword is turned downwards to show that he will further the Christian church with words, not war. He holds the key to the gates of heaven in his other hand and around his neck is a crucifix, now the symbol of the Christian church.

The Bible passage ends with the question, 'What does all this mean?' No answer is offered, but we too might well ask, 'Well, what does *it all mean?'*

 Looking at the picture

◈ What is the artist telling us by the way he has painted the top of this picture?

◈ What might be meant by the flames that touch the disciples?

◈ What is the response of the disciple on the far right?

◈ Who might the woman be?

◈ What is going through the mind of the child?

Lesson Planning Guide for Key Stage Two

Programmes of study

YEARS 3 AND 4

1	Birth	p. 75	One unit	• What is your experience of the birth of a baby? • What do you know about your own birth or adoption? • How are births celebrated in your family?	Events 1, 2 and 3
2	Jesus the Jew	pp. 76-78	Two units + 2 worksheets	• What do parents do when their children are born? • What changes happen in us as we grow up? • Do Jews use the temple today?	Events 5 and 6
3	Symbols	pp. 79-80	One unit + worksheet	• Why do we use symbols?	Events 6, 11, 16 and 18
4	Friends	p. 81	One unit	• Why are friends important to us?	Event 9
5	Miracles	p. 82	One unit	• What are miracles?	Event 10
6	Festivals (Holy Week)	pp. 83-85	One unit + worksheet	• How do Christians remember Jesus' final week in Jerusalem?	Events 14, 15, 16, 19 and 20
7	Visions	p. 86	One unit	• Are there some moments in life that are puzzling and amazing?	Event 13

YEARS 5 AND 6

1	Birth	pp. 87-90	Two units + worksheet	• What do these stories of Jesus' birth tell us about Christian beliefs? • Why are there variations between the Bible stories of the nativity and the one most people know?	Events 1, 2 and 3
2	Trust	pp. 91-92	Two units	• How would Mary have felt when this unexpected announcement happened? • What do we do when we are afraid?	Events 1 and 11
3	Good and evil	p. 93	Two units	• How do we choose between right and wrong? • Is it right never to fight back?	Events 8 and 17
4	Festivals (Pentecost)	p. 94	One unit	• What do Christians believe about the Holy Spirit?	Event 22
5	Encountering mystery	p. 95	Two units	• What is happening in this story about healing? • Was Jesus right to go on trusting that God would forgive people?	Events 10 and 19
6	Faith and doubt	p. 96	One unit	• Is it wrong to ask questions about what people believe?	Events 20 and 21

Lesson plans: Years 3 and 4

PROGRAMME OF STUDY 1:

BIRTH

 Aim of this unit

This unit asks pupils to reflect on their experience of the birth of children, and to make connections between this and the nativity story. It draws on their previous knowledge of the nativity story, and seeks to help them understand the meaning of this story for Christians.

> **USE EVENTS 1, 2 AND 3.**
>
> **Event 1: The birth of Jesus is announced**
> LUKE 1:26–31
>
> **Joseph dreams**
> MATTHEW 1:18–21
>
> **Event 2: The birth of Jesus**
> LUKE 2:1–19
>
> **Event 3: The wise men**
> MATTHEW 2:1–12

 Key questions

❍ What is your experience of the birth of a baby?

❍ What do you know about your own birth or adoption?

❍ How are births celebrated in your family?

 Activities

Ensure that children understand the narrative and have seen the pictures.

❍ What do families do as they prepare for the birth of a baby?

❍ What happens when a baby has been born?

Pupils could be encouraged to talk or write about the birth of a brother or sister or cousin. Some pupils may have pictures of their own birth or adoption and may have their own accounts of this experience. Make a collection of the pictures. Write the accounts, and compare how different families respond.

Read the story of Jesus' birth again. How do the Bible accounts of the preparation for Jesus' birth differ from each other?

> Jesus was born into a risky situation and he was temporarily homeless. Christians believe that because Jesus was born in this way, they must never forget people who are homeless and at risk.

❍ Find out about the work that Christians do among homeless people and refugees. Pupils could send to Christian Aid for some information.

 Assessment of this unit

Learning *about*
❍ Can pupils make links between the story of Jesus' birth and some Christian beliefs about him?

Learning *from*
❍ Can pupils compare aspects of their own experiences and feelings to the situations of others?

> **Getting ready for the birth of a baby: A survey**
>
> Questions to be asked at home:
>
> ❍ What would you like best, for a baby to be born at home or in a hospital?
>
> ❍ Would you go on a long journey, either walking or on the back of a donkey, just before a baby is to be born?
>
> ❍ What do you need to have ready at home for a baby, to look after her/him properly?
>
> ❍ What do you think is the greatest danger for a newborn baby?

PROGRAMME OF STUDY 2:

JESUS THE JEW

 ## Aim of these units

Pupils will learn some Jewish customs of the first century AD and reflect on their own experiences of childhood and growth. They will identify the customs of different faiths.

USE EVENTS 5 AND 6.

1. Event 5: Simeon praises the Lord
LUKE 2:22–35

 ## Key question

○ What do parents do when their children are born?

 ## Activities

Ensure that children understand the narrative and have seen the picture.

Ask the children to find out about what religious customs their parents followed when they were born. This question may yield family parties, baptism, Jewish, Muslim or other faith celebrations, or these latter can be referred to if they are not within the experience of the class. Groups can research a number of different customs, and the findings can be presented to the whole class.

Make the point that Jesus was born as a Jew. He was not baptized until he was thirty. Christian baptism recalls the baptism of Jesus, and not the presentation of Jesus in the temple. Increasing numbers of Christians are baptized as adults and there is a growing practice of thanksgiving for the birth of babies, with baptism and (within the Anglican tradition) confirmation taking place later.

2. Event 6: The boy Jesus in the temple
LUKE 2:41–52

 ## Key question

○ What changes happen in us as we grow up?

 ## Activities

Ensure that children understand the narrative and have seen the picture.

Look at the picture and ask the children how Jesus felt, and what Mary must have felt like. Look at Jesus' reply. Is this hurtful to Mary? Ask the children if they have had similar experiences.

○ Why do our parents have rules for us, and why do they make sure we keep the rules?

○ What do we have to do to help our parents to know that we can be trusted?

 ## Extension activity

○ Do Jews use the temple today?

The Jewish temple was pulled down by the Romans in AD 70 and never rebuilt, but the foundation wall of the temple is still standing and is known as the Western Wall. It has become a very important Jewish place of prayer and pilgrimage. When Jews pray here, they remember the temple and its beauty, and they write prayers and requests to God on little pieces of paper and stick them into the cracks between the stones on the wall.

○ What prayers might you want to put on to a piece of paper and put into the temple wall? Think about this, and make a collection of the prayers of everyone in the class.

 ## Assessment of these units

Learning *about*
○ Can pupils make links between what they know of Jesus and his Jewish background?

○ Can pupils describe some Jewish and Christian customs at the birth of a baby, and know the difference?

Learning *from*
○ Can pupils understand the religious practices of others?

○ Can pupils describe some religious practices and some of the feelings associated with them?

○ Can pupils identify and talk about some difficult moments of conflict with friends and family?

Celebrating the birth of a baby

What happened to me when I was born?
Picture and description

Find out what happens at a Christian baptism.
Picture and writing

Find out the customs of another world faith at the birth of a new baby.
Pictures and writing

Family rules

Write out the important rules in your family.

What rules would you give yourself, if you could choose?

If you had to look after a child younger than yourself for a day, what rules do you think you would set them?

What might Jesus have said in his defence when Mary told him that he had been missing and she and Joseph were worried?

PROGRAMME OF STUDY 3:
SYMBOLS

 ## Aim of this unit

In this unit, pupils will make links between religious symbols, language and stories, and the beliefs that underlie them.

USE EVENTS 6, 11, 16 AND 18.

Event 6: The boy Jesus in the temple
LUKE 2:41–52

Event 11: Jesus calms a storm
LUKE 8:22–25

Event 16: The Lord's Supper
MATTHEW 26:20–30

Event 18: Pilate questions Jesus
MATTHEW 27:11–26

 ## Key question

○ Why do we use symbols?

 ## Activities

Ensure that children understand the narrative and have seen the pictures.

Symbols in everyday life

Look at the picture, *Jesus calms a storm*.

○ What does the flag at the top mean? It is the maritime signal for 'In need of assistance'.

○ Why do sailors use flags for signals? Find out more about the meaning of flags at sea.

○ What other ways do we have of communicating to each other without spoken or written words? Make a list. (This would include sign language, morse code, road signs, signs around the school, symbols on maps.)

Symbols in pictures and paintings

Artists use symbols to tell us a story in their pictures. Look at the picture, *Jesus calms a storm*. What symbols does the artist use to tell us that the disciples are lonely and in danger? Look at the picture, *Pilate questions Jesus*. What does the artist put into this picture to help us to understand the atmosphere of the room where Jesus is on trial?

Religious symbols

Look at the picture, *The boy Jesus in the temple*.

Like symbols in everyday life, religious symbols represent important ideas and understandings. There are several different uses of symbols in this picture. The crook is a symbol of religious authority. The book is a symbol of the scriptures. (In Jesus' time, the scriptures would have been written on scrolls.) The beads symbolize Jesus as someone who spends time in prayer. (Prayer beads are not a Jewish tradition.) The lamp is a religious symbol for the presence of God. Mary carries a water bottle to tell us of her journey. The cockerel and spilt seed are reminders of a visit Jesus will make to the temple when he is older. The dove is a sign of the Holy Spirit.

Using this understanding, look through the other paintings, and see what different symbols the artist uses. Make a list.

 ## Assessment of this unit

Learning *about*
○ Can pupils make links between some key religious symbols and the meanings and beliefs that underlie them?

○ Can pupils make links between a painting and the story it illustrates?

Learning *from*
○ Can pupils express their own feelings in a variety of symbolic ways—for example, through music, painting and dance?

Symbols

Symbols in everyday life

Look around your classroom. What symbols are there in it? Would it be helpful to have other symbols here to help children find things or put things away?

Draw the symbols and discuss them with your teacher.

Look around the school. Would it be helpful to visitors to have some symbols to show them the way? Are there other symbols that could be helpful?

Draw them and write about it.

Religious symbols

Find some books on religion and research six different religious symbols. Draw them here and give their meaning.

Many saints have symbols. Find some pictures of saints and draw their symbols.

Could you invent a symbol for yourself? Draw this and explain why you have chosen this particular symbol.

PROGRAMME OF STUDY 4:
FRIENDS

Aim of this unit

This unit will ask children to reflect on friendship and why friends are important to us. In the light of that experience, they will explore why the first disciples trusted Jesus enough to follow him.

> **USE EVENT 9.**
>
> **Event 9: Jesus chooses his first disciples**
> LUKE 5:1–11

Key question

○ Why are friends important to us?

Discussion

Ask the children to think about friendship. Ask them to complete the sentence 'I like my friends because…'. Make a list of all the comments on a sheet of paper.

Talk about the fishermen on Galilee. Fishing was a difficult job and sometimes a dangerous one. Storms could blow up suddenly on the lake and a small boat could easily be in trouble. If you worked together it was important to be able to trust each other. In the story, when Peter's boat is full, he knows he can call to his friends and they will be looking out for him. Has anyone needed to trust a friend to help them when there was no one else around?

What does the word 'trust' mean? Make a list of children's suggestions.

A dictionary definition of trust says: 'a quality in someone that can be relied on'. When Jesus asked the three friends to follow him, they did not know him very well, but they left everything behind to be with him. What do you think they saw in Jesus, or felt about him, that made them able to do this? Collect the suggestions that children make.

Activities

Ensure that children understand the narrative and have seen the picture.

○ Look up the word 'friendship' in two or three dictionaries and write down the definitions. Then look up the word 'trust' and write down the definitions. Now write what you think these words mean, and perhaps give some examples from your own experience.

○ Imagine you are Peter, and Jesus has just said to you, 'Leave everything and follow me!' What goes through your mind? What do you think about? Try to imagine the contrast between your home and the fact that you know Jesus has no regular place to stay. What might it be like to travel with him, with the crowds following?

Assessment of this unit

Learning *about*
○ Are children able to suggest meanings for religious language?

Learning *from*
○ Are they able to make a link between their experience and the religious experience behind this story?

○ Are they able to compare their experience with that of others?

PROGRAMME OF STUDY 5:
MIRACLES

 Aim of this unit

In this unit, pupils will be encouraged to ask questions about an unusual event, and to compare their own ideas with those of others. They will learn some key ideas and teachings associated with Jesus.

USE EVENT 10.

Event 10: Jesus heals a man
MATTHEW 8:1–4

 Key question

○ What are miracles?

 Discussion

Look at the picture. How did people in the ancient world behave towards those with a skin disease? (See notes on page 46.) How do we treat people who are sick? Are we better than people in the ancient world? When Jesus touched this man, he was doing something very unusual. He taught people to accept each other and not put up barriers. He said that we must treat other people as we would like to be treated ourselves. What do you think about this? Is it possible for us to do this?

○ What do you think a miracle is? Is it something we don't understand now, but might understand one day? Would it have seemed a miracle to a lonely man when he was welcomed and touched by Jesus? Can you think of some changes in people's lives that they might call miracles?

○ Jesus healed a number of people, including this man, just by a touch. Is this possible?

Christians believe that Jesus came to help people live better lives. They also believe that the energy of God enabled him to do some unusual things. Sometimes, nowadays, people find they are healed when they pray, or when a priest or healer touches them in the name of Jesus. Many people would not accept that this is possible.

Christians would say that this kind of healing is not common, and it is always unexpected, but it does happen from time to time. Prayer for people who are unwell is very important for Christians. Christians also believe that in a world made by God we should learn about the reasons for illnesses, and how they can be cured through medicine and better preventative action.

 Activities

Ensure that children understand the narrative and have seen the picture.

○ Write down what you have learned about miracles from this discussion. At the end, explain what your own opinion is, and try to make clear the reasons why you think as you do.

 Assessment of this unit

Learning *about*
○ Are pupils able to describe the attitude of Christians towards miracles?

○ Are pupils able to understand that we use the word 'miracle' in a variety of ways?

Learning *from*
○ Can pupils respond sensitively to the experiences and feelings of others, particularly those who have faith?

○ Can pupils respond sensitively to a code of conduct that encourages us to treat others as we would like to be treated ourselves?

○ Do pupils realize that some questions about faith are difficult to answer?

PROGRAMME OF STUDY 6:
FESTIVALS (HOLY WEEK)

 Aim of this unit

This unit will explore the ways in which Christians remember and celebrate the events of Holy Week, and enable pupils to understand what lies behind them.

> **USE EVENTS 14, 15, 16, 19 AND 20.**
>
> **Event 14: Jesus enters Jerusalem**
> MATTHEW 21:1–11
>
> **Event 15: Jesus washes the feet of his disciples**
> JOHN 13:4–12
>
> **Event 16: The Lord's Supper**
> MATTHEW 26:20–30
>
> **Event 19: Jesus is nailed to a cross**
> MATTHEW 27:31–54
>
> **Event 20: Jesus is alive**
> MARK 16:1–8

 Key question

○ How do Christians remember Jesus' final week in Jerusalem?

 Activities

Ensure that children understand the narrative and have seen the pictures.

○ Read the story of Holy Week, with reference to the pictures. Allow pupils to react to the story in their own way. How do they react to the behaviour of the disciples? How would they have behaved? Could we do something like this to a person who has not done anything wrong today? Do the children think that Jesus' trust in God helped him on the cross?

○ Draw the pupils' attention to the way Jesus behaves throughout the events of Holy Week. Although he faces cruelty and real pain, he does not retaliate, verbally or by action. He seems to look at the events around him with a deep understanding of the powerlessness of the people who are condemning him and mistreating him.

> For Christians, Jesus on the cross reveals the true extent of God's love for us. God seeks to change our worst nature by loving us. We can either accept this or reject it. For this reason Christians are deeply concerned by the use of violence, even for good reasons.

Background

Christians set aside the week leading up to Easter to remember all of the different events that took place in Jerusalem at the time of the crucifixion and resurrection. There are many different ways in which this is done. Some churches and denominations do it very simply, with prayers and readings. Others do so with centuries-old customs, and with music and drama. The practice varies across the many different cultures of Christianity. Christians in South India, for example, whose church was founded in the fifth century, celebrate Easter with a procession of elephants.

Much Holy Week practice in Western Christianity is derived from the experience of pilgrims to Jerusalem in the fourth century. It was about this time that free passage around the Mediterranean became possible, and a number of people made the journey. There is historical record of processions and services around the principal places associated with this week, which were part of a natural desire by Christians to re-enact the final events of Jesus' life. Returning pilgrims influenced the practice of their local churches, which was eventually standardized into a common practice.

At the heart of all the celebrations is a common theme. Worshippers seek to understand the way in which, during this week, everything that Jesus taught and embodied comes into focus. For Christians, Holy Week underlines the way of living taught by Jesus, with its emphasis on openness to others, generosity and forgiveness. He models a way of responding lovingly when faced with adversity and evil, entering the heart of it without any concessions to its power.

Easter speaks of the new life, given unexpectedly by God, often the other side of negative experience, which lies at the heart of all Christian commitment. From Easter Day we derive our current Sunday (for Christians, the first day of the week), with its regular pattern of worship, itself based on the resurrection. Maundy Thursday is the basis for the Holy Communion service, known also as the Lord's Supper, the Eucharist or the Mass, which, for many churches, is the principal act of Sunday worship.

The different customs of Holy Week can be found in a number of reference books. The list below gives a general outline. The worksheet is designed to bring together story, narrative and some Christian practice and symbolism. Pupils should research what happens in a local church, and perhaps someone from that church could visit to talk about their celebrations. In answering the worksheet, it would be important to reflect this. Children should know local practice but also respect the different traditions within the Christian church.

THE CELEBRATION OF HOLY WEEK

Palm Sunday

Sometimes, to remember Jesus' entry into Jerusalem, a donkey leads a procession, with people carrying palm branches or pussy willow. Palm crosses are given out. The whole of the narrative of this week, up to Good Friday, is read from one of the Gospels. In churches where special robes are worn, called vestments, purple is used to underline the solemn nature of the week.

Maundy Thursday

Jesus' last meal with his disciples is remembered in a number of different ways. This could be a simple service of Holy Communion. Often it is a more elaborate service, with white vestments and songs of celebration. This service is seen as a gift to his followers by Jesus, for which there is a sense of gratitude. In some churches, the priest washes the feet of twelve members of the congregation. At the end of the service, the church ornaments are taken out, and the altars are stripped bare, as a symbol of Jesus' arrest and trial. Sometimes some wafers from the Holy Communion are kept on a small side altar, decorated with flowers. People pray here, observing the time of Jesus' trial.

Good Friday

Jesus was on the cross from 12.00 midday until 3.00pm, when he died. This is the usual time of Good Friday services. Some churches hold a meditation for the whole of this time. Others observe a traditional service in which the narrative of the trial and crucifixion is read again, and a cross is carried into the church and held up as a reminder of the event. There is a growing custom of different churches coming together for a procession or a united service. Young Christians often build a small garden, with crosses and a tomb. On Good Friday it is simple and bare.

Holy Saturday

There are no services on this day, when the church remembers Jesus in the grave. Preparations are made for Easter. Special food is cooked. Perhaps the Easter Vigil service described below is held in the evening.

Easter Day

The Easter Vigil comes from the services held around the tomb of Jesus in the Church of the Resurrection in Jerusalem. It begins very early in the morning (as described in the Gospels) outside the church with the lighting of a new fire—a symbol of the new life Jesus brings. From this the Easter candle is lit and carried into the darkened church. This is the light of Christ, shining in the darkness. Each person present lights a candle from the Easter candle, spreading out until the whole church is lit. The church is decorated with flowers. White or sometimes gold vestments are worn. There are readings and the renewal of the vows that were taken at baptism. Then there is a joyful celebration of the Holy Communion, and special hymns are sung. The Easter garden is decorated with flowers. In some churches the Easter candle is lit at the start of the main service of the day. The candle is decorated and has the date of the year on it. It is often kept by the font and lit at baptisms during the rest of the year.

 Assessment of this unit

Learning *about*

○ Can pupils describe the key events of Holy Week?

○ Can pupils make links between the events of Holy Week and the practice of Christians today?

Learning *from*

○ Can pupils talk about the ways we behave towards people who are victims?

○ Can they make links between some of their own values and feelings and those of people of faith?

Finding out about Holy Week

Day of the week	What did Jesus do on this day?	How do Christians remember this?	Draw one thing to do with this day. It could be a symbol of the day.
Palm Sunday			
Maundy Thursday			
Good Friday			
Saturday			
Easter Day			

PROGRAMME OF STUDY 7:
VISIONS

 ## Aim of this unit

This unit will ask pupils to consider a dramatic encounter with Jesus which challenged the disciples' understanding. It will ask pupils to reflect on their own experience, and how they might accommodate the idea of mystery.

> **USE EVENT 13.**
>
> **Event 13: The true glory of Jesus**
> LUKE 9:28–36

 ## Key question

○ Are there some moments in life that are puzzling and amazing?

 ## Discussion

Look at the picture. Imagine what it must have been like to be the disciples. They knew Jesus very well, but now he looks quite different. They are not frightened; they are just very puzzled and amazed. It is a wonderful moment. From now on, whenever they listen to him and talk with him, they will remember this about him. So his words will matter more to them, and he will seem greater to them than ever before.

○ Have you ever seen anything that made you stop and think?

○ Has some music ever made you gasp and think 'how wonderful!'

○ Do you ever look up at the stars and see how big the world is and realize how small we are?

○ Have you ever stopped to look at a beautiful sunset?

○ Have you ever looked at something and wanted to go on looking at it because it is so special?

Sometimes we think we understand everything about life. But we don't, and perhaps we never will. Sometimes we have our eyes open to these moments, but perhaps we miss many moments like this because we are too busy thinking about ourselves, or we think we know and understand everything.

> Christians believe that God made the world and is always present in it in a mysterious and wonderful way. They try to recognize the presence of God in all the people and events around them.

 ## Activities

Ensure that children understand the narrative and have seen the picture.
Children might:

○ Write a poem about a moment that has been very special for them—perhaps a beautiful sunset or a favourite piece of music.

○ Imagine what it must have been like to be one of the disciples, seeing someone you knew become changed and wonderful before your eyes.

○ Write a poem about how it would be if we always kept our eyes open for special moments.

 ## Assessment of this unit

Learning *about*

○ Can pupils retell this story and describe the significance of Jesus for the disciples?

Learning *from*

○ Can pupils compare aspects of their own deeper experiences with the experiences of others?

Lesson plans: Years 5 and 6

PROGRAMME OF STUDY 1:
BIRTH

Aim of these units

The aim of this unit is to explore the Christian belief that the nativity story points to a God who is deeply concerned with human affairs. It also aims to help pupils understand the ways in which religious narratives become part of a cultural inheritance, and are elaborated as they do so. It encourages a close study of the biblical texts.

USE EVENTS 1, 2 AND 3.

Event 1: The birth of Jesus is announced
LUKE 1:26–31

Joseph dreams
MATTHEW 1:18–21

Event 2: The birth of Jesus
LUKE 2:1–19

Event 3: The wise men
MATTHEW 2:1–12

---

1. THE MEANING OF THE STORY

Key question

○ What do these stories of Jesus' birth tell us about Christian beliefs?

Activities

Ensure that children understand the narrative and have seen the pictures.

○ Read the accounts in Matthew and Luke. If you were poor and lived under a military government, what would you most hope for from God?

○ What must Mary have felt like?

○ Do you think that being born in a stable would have made any difference to Jesus' attitude to people?

○ What message might God want to send to people in the world today? Thinking about that, where might Jesus be born today, and what might the stories about his birth tell us?

○ Write a modern nativity story.

○ Make models of the kinds of houses Jesus might be born in today—for example, a concrete flat in Palestine or a shanty house in South Africa, and set up a nativity scene that reflects this.

2. DIFFERENT CHRISTMAS STORIES

 Key question

○ Why are there variations between the Bible stories of the nativity and the one most people know?

 Activities

Ensure that children understand the narrative and have seen the pictures.

○ Divide the children into groups and ask them to note down the details of the Christmas story that they know. Then hand out the worksheet: 'Comparing three accounts of Jesus' birth'. Allow pupils time to work out their own reasons for the differences.

Point to note: In the final discussion, teachers might explain that the two Gospel accounts were written in different places by authors who possibly drew on different local stories. In addition, each author has a particular 'view' about Jesus: Matthew saw him as a light to the whole world (hence the travellers), while Luke always portrays him as someone deeply concerned with the poor (hence the shepherds). So far as we know, they did not see each other's account and they certainly did not intend these details to fit together in the way they have been woven together by tradition. But both are agreed on the central issue of the birth of Jesus, and the roles of Mary and Joseph in it. It is also true that in oral traditions stories tend to gain added detail as they are told and retold.

○ Look at other paintings of the Christmas story. In each case, what is the artist trying to tell us? In what ways do they differ from the Bible story? How would the pupils explain all these differences?

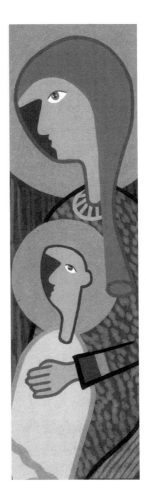

 Assessment of these units

Learning *about*

○ Are pupils aware of the differences between Luke's and Matthew's accounts of the birth?

○ Can pupils show how the stories of Christmas express Christian ideas and beliefs?

Learning *from*

○ Can pupils suggest answers to difficult problems out of their own experience?

○ Do pupils begin to understand some of the moral and religious issues raised by the nativity story?

Comparing three accounts of Jesus' birth —the one we know and the ones told by Matthew and Luke.

First, cover up the accounts on the next sheet and, with a partner, discuss what you know about the birth of Jesus.

> Write down on a piece of paper the main characters and places.
> Who were Jesus' parents?
> What happened around his birth?
> Where was he born?
> Who visited him?

Comparing three accounts of Jesus' birth —
the one we know and the ones told by Matthew and Luke.

Now read these accounts.

Matthew's account
MATTHEW 2:1–12

When Jesus was born in the village of Bethlehem in Judea, Herod was king. During this time some wise men from the east came to Jerusalem and said, 'Where is the child born to be king of the Jews? We saw his star in the east and have come to worship him.'

When King Herod heard about this, he was worried, and so was everyone else in Jerusalem. Herod brought together the chief priests and the teachers of the Law of Moses and asked them, 'Where will the Messiah be born?'

They told him, 'He will be born in Bethlehem, just as the prophet wrote...'

Herod secretly called in the wise men and asked them when they had first seen the star. He told them, 'Go to Bethlehem and search carefully for the child. As soon as you find him, let me know. I want to go and worship him too.'

The wise men listened to what the king said and then left. And the star they had seen in the east went on ahead of them until it stopped over the place where the child was. They were thrilled and excited to see the star.

When the men went into the house and saw the child with Mary, his mother, they knelt down and worshipped him. They took out their gifts of gold, frankincense and myrrh and gave them to him. Later they were warned in a dream not to return to Herod, and they went back home by another road.

Luke's account
LUKE 2:1–16

About that time Emperor Augustus gave orders for the names of all the people to be listed in record books... Everyone had to go to their own home town to be listed. So Joseph had to leave Nazareth in Galilee and go to Bethlehem in Judea. Long ago Bethlehem had been King David's home town, and Joseph went there because he was from David's family.

Mary was engaged to Joseph and travelled with him to Bethlehem. She was soon going to have a baby, and while they were there, she gave birth to her firstborn son. She dressed him in baby clothes and laid him on a bed of hay, because there was no room for them in the inn.

That night in the fields near Bethlehem some shepherds were guarding their sheep. All at once the angel came down to them from the Lord, and the brightness of the Lord's glory flashed around them. The shepherds were frightened. But the angel said, 'Don't be afraid! I have good news for you, which will make everyone happy. This very day in King David's home town a Saviour was born for you. He is Christ the Lord. You will know who he is, because you will find him dressed in baby clothes and lying on a bed of hay.'

Suddenly many other angels came down from heaven and joined in praising God. They said: 'Praise to God in heaven! Peace on earth to everyone who pleases God.'

After the angels had left and gone back to heaven, the shepherds said to each other, 'Let's go to Bethlehem and see what the Lord has told us about.' They hurried off and found Mary and Joseph, and they saw the baby lying in a bed of hay.

When you have read these accounts, get four crayons—red, blue, green and yellow. Work on these two passages and your own notes. Across the three:

IN RED   underline: Mary, Joseph, Jesus, Bethlehem, Law of Moses.

IN BLUE   underline: Herod, Jerusalem, wise men. Who wrote about *three* wise men?

IN GREEN   underline: angels, shepherds, baby clothes, bed of hay ('manger' would count).

IN YELLOW   underline: donkey, ox, ass, stable, camels, innkeeper.

Now look at all three accounts. Is Matthew's account the same as Luke's? What are the differences? How different is your account? What do all the accounts agree about? Talk about why these accounts may be a mixture of similar and different events.

 Reproduced with permission from *The Life of Jesus Teacher's Guide* published by BRF 2004 (1 84101 331 5)

PROGRAMME OF STUDY 2:
TRUST

Aim of these units

The aim of the unit is to explore some of the reactions of Jesus' contemporaries to the events that they found themselves in. Pupils will be asked to look at some of the puzzling questions that surround Jesus, and explore the ideas of fear and trust.

> **USE EVENTS I AND II.**
>
> **Event I: The birth of Jesus is announced**
> Luke 1:26–31
>
> **Joseph dreams**
> Matthew 1:18–21
>
> **Event II: Jesus calms a storm**
> Luke 8:22–25

I. THE BIRTH OF JESUS IS ANNOUNCED

Key question

○ How would Mary have felt when this unexpected announcement happened?

Discussion

Think about the story. What *feelings* might Mary have had?

○ Do you think she really believed it was possible for this to happen?

○ What could she have done? List the different things that were possible.

There are a lot of books in which unexpected things happen to people—for example, Philip Pullman's book *Northern Lights*. We enjoy reading these stories. Can we learn something from stories that tell us something unexpected and unusual?

Unexpected things happen to people in real life too, which can change the course of people's lives. Can you find out about any of these experiences?

A question to think about
Are we ready for unexpected things to happen? We get up in the morning… go to school… go home… see our friends… go to bed. Life is what we expect it to be. But is it possible that there is far more to life than we ever notice? Sometimes children and adults experience a moment when everything seems wonderful,

alive and full of significance. Has this ever happened to you? If not, could it?

○ Do you think this story of Mary is trying to tell us something very important?

○ Are people who 'have a religious faith' ready to live in a world that is much larger and more mysterious than we can just see with our eyes?

> Christians believe that God sometimes makes clear to them what they have to do. They try to trust God, even if, like Mary, what is asked of them is unexpected and difficult.

Activities

Ensure that children understand the narrative and have seen the picture.

○ Think about Mary and how she must have felt. Write a poem or a piece of prose to describe those feelings.

○ Imagine that you are on a desert island with your friends. They turn to you and ask you to be the leader of the group. What are your thoughts? How do you feel? Could you do this? What will you do?

2. JESUS CALMS A STORM

 Key question

○ What do we do when we are afraid?

 Activities

Ensure that children understand the narrative and have seen the picture.

○ What is the most frightening situation you have experienced? When we are frightened, do we always do the right thing? If we are frightened, does it help to be with someone who is not frightened at all? Have you ever been frightened, and then someone has explained the situation to you and your fear has gone away? In the picture and the story, what makes the disciples calm down?

○ Imagine yourself on a walk with someone younger than yourself, when they become frightened because they are away from home. How would you calm them?

 Some puzzling questions

What do we mean when we use the word 'trust'? Whom do you trust most of all? What is it about someone that makes you feel they can be trusted? Is part of what we mean by the word 'fear' the feeling that we are alone and that there is no one around that we can 'trust'?

 Activities

○ Read the story again, and ask what the disciples might have learned about Jesus as a result of the storm.

○ Imagine you are in a boat in a terrible storm, a long way from land. Everyone is panicking, but you think that you can see a way to save everyone. What do you do? Write about this.

○ Imagine that you are in charge of a younger child at home, and they become worried and anxious. Perhaps you have had this experience? What do you say to reassure them?

○ Think about the word 'trust', about the people you can trust, and what the word means. Then write a poem to explain your feelings.

Assessment of these units

Learning *about*

○ Can pupils talk about meanings of these key Gospel stories?

○ Can pupils talk about stories they have enjoyed, in which unexpected and out-of-the-ordinary events happen?

○ Do pupils understand that these and other stories point to Jesus as someone around whom extraordinary things happened?

Learning *from*

○ Are pupils able to talk about their own responses to these stories?

○ Are they alert to puzzling experiences in their own lives?

○ Can they make an informed response to these experiences?

PROGRAMME OF STUDY 3:
GOOD AND EVIL

 Aim of these units

Pupils will encounter some key beliefs of Christians, and begin to explore how these key teachings make a difference to the lives of individuals.

> **USE EVENTS 8 AND 17.**
>
> **Event 8: The temptations of Jesus**
> MATTHEW 4:1–11
>
> **Event 17: Jesus is arrested**
> MATTHEW 26:47–56

1. THE TEMPTATIONS OF JESUS

 Key question

○ How do we choose between right and wrong?

 Discussion

Read the story and the background commentary on it. It is important to understand that these temptations are things that promise to do good in the long run. It is the *means* of doing good that Jesus rejects in each case. Ensure that children understand the narrative and have seen the picture.

Try setting up a discussion with a friend. Your friend's job is to persuade you to do something you think you should not do. Take it in turns to do this. Here are some situations:

○ You see someone being bullied at school. You know that the rule is to report it at once to a teacher, but you are tempted to do something yourself. Look at both viewpoints.

○ Imagine that you have met a family with young children. They are really hungry, and have no money. Nearby you see a shop with some food. The shopkeeper has his back turned. You could easily steal some food for these people, and he would not notice. Would it be right to do this? Go through the arguments for and against.

○ A friend of yours is in trouble with a teacher. He is accused of having started some trouble. He probably is innocent, but he cannot prove it. To help him out, you say (untruthfully) that at the time of the incident he was somewhere else with you. Is it right to do this or not?

○ Can you think of other situations like this where you might try to do something good by doing something wrong?

> Christians believe that good results can only come from good actions. They believe that we should be truthful to the deepest and best motives within us, whatever the circumstances. Do you agree with this?

2. JESUS IS ARRESTED

 Key question

○ Is it right never to fight back?

 Discussion

Ensure that children understand the narrative and have seen the picture.

Think about the scene in the picture. If Jesus' disciples had stayed to protect him, they could probably have defended him, at least for a while. Peter makes an attempt, but Jesus tells him it is wrong to use a sword. Is Jesus right? What would you have done? Do you think it is right never to fight back, even if we are wrongly attacked?

In India, when people were fighting for independence, they refused to cooperate with the rulers but they did so without fighting. It was called non-violent resistance. Sometimes the police were very brutal, but even then the Indian people did not respond. In the end, the authorities had to give up and leave. They had no weapons against non-violence. Do you think that this would be a better way of solving problems than fighting?

○ Discuss this. Write down your thoughts about Jesus' way of non-violence, and his instruction to love our enemies and do good to those who hate us. What do you think of this? Is it practical?

 Assessment of these units

Learning *about*
○ Are pupils able to describe some key Christian beliefs after studying this unit?

○ Are pupils able to make an informed response to this religious teaching?

Learning *from*
○ Can pupils talk about and recognize the full range of our behaviour to others?

○ Are pupils able to make a personal response to the moral issues involved in this lesson?

PROGRAMME OF STUDY 4:

FESTIVALS (PENTECOST)

 ### Aim of this unit

This unit introduces pupils to a key Christian belief, encourages them to ask questions about a significant aspect of Christian experience and asks pupils to reflect on their own experiences.

> **USE EVENT 22.**
>
> **Event 22: The coming of the Holy Spirit**
> ACTS 2:1–12

PENTECOST

 ### Key question

○ What do Christians believe about the Holy Spirit?

 ### Activities

Ensure that children understand the narrative and have seen the picture.

○ Look at the picture and read the account from Acts. Encourage the children to imagine what it would have been like to stand in the place of the boy in the picture. What would he see and hear? How would the disciples feel?

○ Ask the children to talk about the most exciting time in their lives. How did they feel? When we feel something strongly, it is often difficult to find words to describe how we feel. If they had to paint a picture to describe how they felt, what colours would they choose? What symbols would they choose?

> Sometimes Christians feel that they are close to the presence of God, and that God is helping them in some way. Some have the experience of 'speaking in tongues', that is praying in another language, even today. It is not usually a time of excitement, as Pentecost was for the disciples. Often it is a very quiet experience. Afterwards they say that they feel stronger, or understand something better.

After Pentecost the disciples began to travel all over the world, telling people about the message of Jesus. Before the coming of the Holy Spirit they had been afraid to do this.

From Pentecost onwards they did not seem concerned if they were thrown into prison.

 ### Some puzzling questions

What is it that makes us feel brave and certain about something? Have there been times when you have done something very difficult—for example, standing up in front of the whole school to say something, or going alone on a very long journey? How did you feel? What is it that makes someone brave and ready to do difficult things?

Think back to the story. The disciples had every reason to be afraid because Jesus had been put to death only a few weeks before. What made them so confident and unafraid?

 ### Activities

Ensure that children understand the narrative and have seen the picture.

○ Paint a picture of Pentecost, using colours that indicate the kinds of feelings the disciples might have had.

○ Think about the word 'courage'. What does it mean? Have there been times when you have seen people you would call courageous? Have you ever been courageous? When you have thought about it, imagine you are giving some advice to the disciples as they go out into a world where they have to be brave. Put your thoughts into a poem or a piece of writing.

 ### Assessment of this unit

Learning *about*
○ Can pupils recount the story of Pentecost and explain the meaning of the symbols used in the story?

Learning *from*
○ Can pupils show an understanding of important events in their own lives?

○ Can they express these events in painting or dance or music?

ENCOUNTERING MYSTERY

 ## Aim of these units

The aim of this unit is to look at some puzzling questions about human experience, and ask if we can learn anything from them.

USE EVENTS 10 AND 19.

Event 10: Jesus heals a man
MATTHEW 8:1–4

Event 19: Jesus is nailed to a cross
MATTHEW 27:31–54

---

1. JESUS HEALS A MAN

 ### Key question

○ What is happening in this story about healing?

 ### Activities

Ensure that children understand the narrative and have seen the picture.

○ Think about this man's feelings. What must it have been like to be thrown out of your family and village, and to have people avoid you?

○ What must it have felt like to be touched by Jesus and see him smiling at you?

○ Do you think that our sad or frightened feelings can sometimes make us ill?

○ Write an account of the feelings this man must have had when he saw Jesus coming and tried to decide what to do.

○ How do we treat people who are ill or lonely?

 ### To think about

Sometimes when people have been really ill, after they recover they say that they have learned a lot during the time that they were suffering from the illness. Do you think that this is possible? What might we learn about during an illness?

2. JESUS IS NAILED TO A CROSS

 ### Key question

○ Was Jesus right to go on trusting that God would forgive people?

 ## Activities

Ensure that children understand the narrative and have seen the picture.

○ Look at the picture. This was a very cruel thing to do to someone, but human beings go on being cruel to each other, even today.

○ What is the best way to stop this? One way would be to have good laws. That is important, and Jesus obviously thought so too. But if people are still brutal, should we bully them in return? Is there a way in which this would make things worse?

○ What makes people do very cruel and evil things?

○ Jesus taught that we should return evil with good. By *never* returning evil, he believed that people, even very cruel people, could be changed. What do you think?

○ If someone was, for example, taken hostage and badly treated, do you think that belief in God would help them survive? What do you think about Jesus' command telling us to love our enemies?

When Nelson Mandela was made a prisoner on Robben Island, he was badly treated by his guards. He decided he would always treat them politely and not respond with a similar hatred, however they treated him. He gradually learned about them and their families, and in the end both he and his guards respected each other.

Have you ever met someone who has made you think about the way you behave towards others?

 ## Discussion

How do we portray people in films, pictures or books to show they are good or evil? Is this right or fair?

 ## Assessment of these units

Learning *about*
○ Can pupils explain how beliefs like these make a difference to the lives of individuals and communities?

Learning *from*
○ Can pupils make an informed response to these ideas and commitments?

PROGRAMME OF STUDY 6:

FAITH AND DOUBT

 Aim of this unit

This unit looks at the central Christian belief in the resurrection. It explores the idea of doubt as a way of reaching the truth, and looks at ways in which the resurrection is spoken about in Christian practice.

> **USE EVENTS 20 AND 21.**
>
> **Event 20: Jesus is alive**
> MARK 16:1–8
>
> **Event 21: Jesus and Thomas**
> JOHN 20:24–29

 Key question

O Is it right to have doubts about religious belief?

RESURRECTION

 Activities

Ensure that children understand the narrative and have seen the pictures.

O Read the story about these pictures.

Jesus is risen from the dead and he has appeared to the disciples, but Thomas was not there. Thomas cannot believe that Jesus was alive because he has seen him die, so he says so. Then Jesus appears again and Thomas recognizes that it really is Jesus because he still has the marks of the nails in his hands. Seeing Jesus, he believes and no longer doubts.

 Discussion

O Is it right to have doubts about religious ideas, or should we just believe them without questioning? If the Bible tells us the story of Thomas who does not believe the other disciples, it must be telling us that it is not wrong to ask questions. Perhaps we have to go on asking questions until we understand.

O It is very hard to believe that someone could be alive if you know that they have died. But is one way of understanding the resurrection to see it as a very powerful picture? Sometimes when things have gone badly wrong, we feel that everything is terrible—

dead, almost. But then, things are put right, and we seem to come alive again. Could this be part of what the disciples mean when they say Jesus is risen from the dead?

O Would it be easier to believe that the disciples had the strong feeling that Jesus was somehow still with them and giving them courage, even though they had seen him die? After the resurrection, they do seem to be better people than they were before.

 A story to think about

The priest of a church in Germany often used to talk with a man who regularly asked him how he could possibly believe that Jesus had risen from the dead. The man could never accept anything that he was told when the priest tried to explain. Always he said that he could not believe such a thing would happen.

Then the man and his wife had a difficult time. They thought that they would have to divorce and the man was very upset.

The priest talked with him, and helped him and his wife to begin to understand each other again. In the end they came to understand each other much better, and both of them felt glad to continue together. A month or so after this, the man came to see the priest. 'You know,' he said, 'I have been thinking. You are right. Jesus is risen from the dead.'

O Do you think that facing problems and not running away from them makes us stronger, and that this might be seen as an experience that is like death and resurrection?

 Assessment of this unit

Learning *about*

O Are pupils able to describe this key belief of the Christian faith?

O Are they able to understand the way Christians use language to talk about this belief?

Learning *from*

O Can pupils ask questions about puzzling experiences?

O Can pupils make an informed response to the values and commitments of other people?